VICTIMS

VICTIMS

A TRUE STORY OF THE CIVIL WAR

★ ★ ★

With a New Preface

Phillip Shaw Paludan

THE UNIVERSITY OF TENNESSEE PRESS
Knoxville

For the McManns, the Shaws, and the Paludans

Library of Congress Cataloging in Publication Data

Paludan, Phillip S., 1938–2007
    Victims: a true story of the Civil War.
    Includes bibliographical references and index.
    1. Shelton Laurel Valley (N.C.)—Massacre, 1863.
2. United States—History—Civil War, 1861–1865—
Prisoners and prisons. I. Title.
F262.M25P34   973.7'33   81.2578

ISBN-13: 978-1-57233-325-3   AACR2
ISBN-10: 1-57233-325-1

CONTENTS

PREFACE
2004

I began work on *Victims: A True Story of the Civil War* in the middle of another book project, which ultimately became *A People's Contest*. The murder of thirteen men and boys by members of the Sixty-fourth North Carolina regiment seemed an interesting sidelight of an inquiry into how wars shape attitudes toward killing. I might have set it on the "to be looked into more later" shelf had echoes of the Vietnam War not begun sounding. The trial of Lieutenant William Calley for the My Lai atrocity intervened. I became intrigued with the question of what happens in the mind and circumstances of men (women don't seem to take part in such things) that allows these horrors to occur.

And so, for a week, or two, or . . . I took some time out to see what had happened there in Appalachia in January 1863. The research almost did itself—each question I had received an answer within a day or two. What exactly had happened? A state newspaper, then a national newspaper, then a report in the *Official Record of the War of the Rebellion,* then some hints in Governor Zebulon Vance's papers, a highly colorized picture in Unionist guide Dan Ellis's memories provided a believable answer. What role did Robert E. Lee's friend General Henry Heth play in giving the murderous orders, and why would he give them? Heth's memoirs, published in the first days of my research, laid out a picture of the type of man Heth was and where he stood in his career when time came to give, or rather to insinuate, the murderous orders to Lt. Col. James Keith and hence to Lt. Col. William Allen. Who were Keith and Allen? That was a harder puzzle, but one answered in part by the manuscript census of 1850 and 1860. A memoir written by a friend of Allen justifying the murders also cast some light.

What kind of world was Western North Carolina in the mid-nineteenth century? Travel accounts, recollections from people who abided in the place, and modern writings, most compellingly by Robert Coles, built a believable world. They were reinforced by wartime reports of the world where "loyalty and treason" blended and often switched sides. What kind of people joined which side? The manuscript census again supplied some answers; talk and correspondence with people from Shelton Laurel narrowed but also deepened my views.

Modern theoretical writing also grabbed me, and that is, in part, the late Clifford S. Griffin's story. For several years Cliff and I had offices side-by-side at the University of Kansas. We taught classes together. We talked constantly about my work and about his. He enjoyed a line from a song by the Eagles—"And take it to the limit, and take it to the limit, one more time. . . ." Cliff always asked for more. For every assertion I made, Cliff's rejoinder might be "Wrong, Phil," but I usually was wrong because I hadn't kept asking why and how. If the historical data only went so far, Cliff said push beyond it. He hit me with H. Stuart Hughes's argument that the job of the historian was not to write only what s/he knew to be true but rather to say nothing that s/he knew to be false. Between and beyond the documents there was the realm of imagination. But it was imagination disciplined by scholarly writing focused on the concepts at stake: What did psychologists say about the "atrocity producing situation"? What did philosophers say about excuses? What did sociologists say about communities? These questions and others like them expanded the historian's domain, informed the evidence, deepened and humanized the story.

And what was that about "story?" What did it mean to write history; how did you write it so that the evidence could be taken to the limit? There were books to be read about narrative, and the significance and value of seeing human experience as a story. Was there something useful about what other storytellers did—fiction writers especially? Historians took some sort of oath to tell the truth about the past—but could the techniques of fiction writers be used to tell more of that truth? Truman Capote, Thomas Wolfe, Norman Mailer, and other writers of "faction" thought they could, so I tried it too. In Norman Maclean's masterpiece, *A River Runs Through It,* there is a conversation between Norman and his father: "'You like to tell true stories, don't you?' he asked, and I answered, 'Yes, I like to tell stories that are true.' Then he asked, 'After you have finished your true stories sometime, why don't you make up a story and the people to go with it? Only then will you understand what happened and why.'" *Victims* isn't made-up, in people or events; but, in the gray area between history and fiction, a truer story might be seen than in history alone. Thanks, Cliff, for pushing the limits.

THE ATROCITY-PRODUCING SITUATION

Fundamentally, *Victims* is about "the atrocity-producing situation," an expression invented by psychiatrist Robert J. Lifton to describe a situation in which soldiers murder and torture civilians. The age, gender, or innocence of the victims is irrelevant, for the killers feel so threatened by their entire environment that every alien thing seems to be a threat. The rules of warfare are suspended, for rules imply the capacity for reason and judgment. In the atrocity-producing situation, terror and/or rage trump self-restraint and any excuse turns loose the beast. Fear of this beast pervades modern critiques of war as well as older musings like Joseph Conrad's *Heart of Darkness.*[1]

But war can be fought within rules, or, at least, respect for rules; and the Civil War fits that category, usually. Even Sherman's march to the sea, which, during the 1960s was foolishly likened to the war in

---

1. See Robert J. Lifton, "American Apocalypse," *The Nation,* Dec. 22, 2003; Ramit Shackam, *Breaking Ranks: Refusing to Serve in the West Bank and Gaza Strip* (New York: Other Press, 2003); Chris Hedges, *War Is a Force That Gives Us Meaning* (New York: Free Press, 2002). See sources on page 96 of the present book.

Vietnam,[2] found soldiers restrained by orders to destroy only property. Very few civilians died, and none was murdered. When soldiers defied orders, they still deferred to moral restraints of their racist age. Rapes were almost unheard of, and these confined to slave women. Rapes of any kind of course are horrible, but the fact that some categories of women were spared, suggest that very little like "total war" or "ethnic cleansing" occurred during this "civil" war.[3]

Sometimes the rules lapsed. Quantrill's raid on Lawrence, Kansas, in August 1863; the massacre at Fort Pillow; the hanging of over two hundred unionists near Gainesville, Texas; George Pickett's execution of twenty-two "deserters" near Kinston, North Carolina, all provide, in various degrees, examples of war at the margins of law. There were other places, Missouri especially, where rules were often suspended.[4] And, in the wartime Southern Appalachian Mountains, the beast also prowled. *Victims* was an effort to find out why.

SCHOLARSHIP ON APPALACHIA AND THE CIVIL WAR

In some ways the search goes on. Historians have explored the events of that mountain world rather thoroughly since I published *Victims* in 1981. They have been attracted to large, regional paradigms about the people and the environment. Perhaps the most compelling question has been "Who were the mountain Unionists, and by extension, which mountaineers were loyal to the Confederacy, and why?" The standard

2. James Reston Jr., *Sherman's March and Vietnam* (New York: Macmillan, 1987).

3. Mark Grimsley, *The Hard Hand of War: Union Military Policy toward Southern Civilians, 1861–1865* (New York: Cambridge University Press, 1995), describes the limitations on military violence in the most often criticized act of the Civil War—Sherman's March. Grimsley's argument is more persuasive than Charles Royster's brilliant *The Destructive War: William Tecumseh Sherman, Stonewall Jackson and the Americans* (New York: Knopf, 1991). For discussion of the limits on civil liberty violations, see Mark E. Neely Jr., *The Fate of liberty* (New York: Oxford University Press, 1991). On the question of total war, see Mark Neely Jr., "Was the Civil War a Total War," *Civil War History* 37 (March 1991): 9–28. Lerone Bennett, *Forced into Glory: Abraham Lincoln's White Dream* (Chicago: Wm. Johnson, 1999), calls Lincoln's policies on colonization "ethnic cleansing."

4. Donald E. Collins, "War Crime or Justice? General George Pickett and the Mass Execution of Deserters in Civil War Kinston, North Carolina," in *The Art of Command in the Civil War,* edited by Steven E. Woodworth (Lawrence: University of Nebraska Press,

answer had been that poorer people of the region, poor in that they owned no slaves, sided with the Union; wealthier people, with the Confederacy. I tried to add another element to this idea by noting that a key factor was connection with the larger Southern economy. People close to towns, rich and poor, were more likely to find the Cotton Kingdom and its tributaries on other varieties of agriculture attractive. Martin Crawford sustained this view of the geography of Unionism and Confederate patriotism in his work on Ashe County, North Carolina, a picture common throughout the whole mountain region. A recent review of the literature supports this view while noting that there were some exceptions.[5]

This scholarship changes my emphasis on the traditional nature of the Unionists of Shelton Laurel, but only by degree. Historians seem to agree that there were places that stayed out of the orbit of the burgeoning Southern economy. In those places Unionism was, in large measure, a reaction to an expanding modernizing cotton culture. Ironically, when viewed in national terms, the Civil War pitted a modernizing North against a more traditional South. But within Dixie these roles were reversed, as in Shelton Laurel.

But loyalty to the old Union could fluctuate. Some parts of the region held their Unionism unflinchingly. Both West Virginia and East Tennessee had a "large group of hard-core loyalists whose commitment to the United States was unalterable." But the sources of this Unionism grew from the "relative absence of slavery and the influence of the Whig party." Party affiliation, in a world so passionate about politics, forged Union bonds. But class seemed less significant.[6]

1998), 50–83; Michael Fellman, *Inside War: The Guerrilla Conflict in Missouri during the Civil War* (New York: Oxford, 1989); Bruce Tap, "These Devils Are Not Fit to Live on God's Earth: War Crimes and the Committee on the Conduct of the War, 1864–1865," *Civil War History* 42 (1996), no. 2: 116–32; Court Carney, "The Contested Image of Nathan Bedford Forrest," *Journal of Southern History* 67 (2001), no. 3: 601–30; Larry Wood, "The Other Anderson: Bloody Bill's Brother Jim," *Missouri Historical Review* 97 (2003), no. 2: 93–108.

5. Martin Crawford, *Ashe County's Civil War: Community and Society in the Appalachian South* (Charlottesville, University of Virginia Press, 2001); Ralph Mann, "Review of Crawford," *American Historical Review* 107 (June 2002): 879–90; Noel Fisher, "Feelin' Mighty Southern: Recent Scholarship on Southern Appalachia in the Civil War," *Civil War History* 47 (2001), no. 4: 334–46.

6. Noel C. Fisher, *War at Every Door: Partisan Politics and Guerrilla Violence in East Tennessee, 1860–1869* (Chapel Hill: University of North Carolina Press, 1997), 179–83.

At the same time, loyalties might change with the fortunes of war. Places that supported the rebellion in early 1861 might switch sides when the Confederacy proved unable to protect them from depriva- tion. Western North Carolina sent a higher percentage of men to the Rebel army than any other part of the state—in the first six months of the conflict. But Unionism emerged when the new nation proved incapable of feeding, clothing, and sheltering both soldiers and civil- ians, and when Richmond began to enforce its draft.[7]

Modern scholarship has given subtlety to a tradition that made the Appalachians of Dixie a bastion of Unionism and a home of pre- modern ways. Historians have shown that Rebels controlled parts of the mountains and that both sides were linked in some ways to a modernizing world.[8] Sections of East Tennessee voted 30 percent for secession and, though allegiance to the Confederacy waned during the conflict, there were still mountaineers who found Jefferson Davis (or more likely Lee) more appealing than Abe Lincoln. In the lower southern highlands there were more of these types. Every section of the mountains had its exceptions to the traditional historiographical rules.[9] And since scholarship lives and dies on exceptions, each his- torian is sure to point out how his or her patch differs from others'. Few have ever made a scholarly career saying "Me, too."

But if scholarship on the mountain war continues to grow as regional study, it has almost ignored the approach taken in *Victims:* that of focusing on a single incident and seeking to understand it in depth. *Victims* is unique in Appalachian studies, and only two works

---

7. Fisher, "Feelin' Mighty Southern," 337.

8. *The Civil War in Appalachia: Collected Essays,* edited by Kenneth W. Noe and Shannon H. Wilson (Knoxville: University of Tennessee Press, 1997), xiv–xv. This work emphasizes how mountain warfare was shaped by larger campaigns as well as by local imperatives.

9. In exploring race questions in the mountains, *Appalachians and Race: The Moun- tain South from Slavery to Segregation,* edited by John Inscoe (Lexington: University Press of Kentucky, 2000), reveals the diversity of the region's loyalties. *After the Backcountry: Rural Life in the Great Valley of Virginia, 1800–1900,* edited by Kenneth E. Koons and Warren R. Hofstra (Knoxville: University of Tennessee Press, 2000) targets one area to reveal a similar integration of traditional and modern experiences and loyalties. An article by Jonathan Sarris, "An Execution in Lumpkin County: Localized Loyalties in North Georgia's Civil War," in *Civil War in Appalachia,* edited by Noe and Wilson, provides use- ful insights on the links between locale and loyalty.

(laying aside battle studies) use that approach in the Civil War years. In *Tainted Breeze: The Great Hanging at Gainesville, Texas, 1862,* Richard McCaslin thoughtfully describes why nearly two hundred suspected Unionists died, but he confines himself to nineteenth-century sources, eschewing modern theories. Winthrop Jordan, in *Tumult and Silence at Second Creek: An Inquiry into a Civil War Slave Conspiracy,* brilliantly excavates the existing evidence to shape a picture of what happened in Adams County, Mississippi, during the summer of 1861. But Jordan does not need to enlist modern psychology and sociology. He is wise enough on his own to provide many modern insights. In Civil War studies, however, I know of no other works beyond Jordan's, McCaslin's, and my own that seek a "thick description" of a single event to study the nature of war at its most extreme.[10]

The genre can be fruitful. In modern times, the My Lai massacre has called forth several works, and Mark Danner's *The Massacre at El Mozote: A Parable of the Cold War* reveals the horror of the Nicaraguan Contra War in a small place. These modern studies have further illuminated how the stories of individual and unique incidents reveal the heart of darkness that lurks when human beings unleash the "dogs of war."[11]

10. Richard B. McCaslin, *Fainted Breeze: The Great Hanging at Gainesville, Texas, 1862* (Baton Rouge: Louisiana State University Press, 1994); Winthrop D. Jordan, *Tumult and Silence at Second Creek: An Inquiry into a Civil War Slave Conspiracy* (Baton Rouge: Louisiana State University Press, 1993). The best introduction to the My Lai literature is *Facing My Lai: Moving Beyond the Massacre,* edited by David Anderson (Lawrence: University Press of Kansas, 1997). For the most recent study of My Lai, see Michael Belnap, *Vietnam War on Trial: The My Lai Massacre* (Lawrence: University Press of Kansas, 2002). Two books on slave rebellions in the prewar period deserve mention: David Robertson, *Denmark Vesey: The Buried Story of America's Largest Slave Rebellion and the Man Who Led It* (New York: Vintage, 1999), and *Nat Turner: Rebellion in History and Memory,* edited by Kenneth Greenberg (New York: Oxford University Press, 2003. In a recent collection of essays, editors John Inscoe and Robert Kinzer point to three studies they admire for showing the "tensions generated within very specific contexts of place and personality, as well as local politics and power struggles." They mention my work, McCaslin's, and Thomas Dyer's *Secret Yankees: The Unionist Circle in Confederate Atlanta* (Baltimore: Johns Hopkins University Press, 1999). See *Enemies of the Country: New Perspectives on Unionists in the Civil War South,* edited by John Inscoe and Robert Kinzer (Athens: University of Georgia Press, 2001), 5–6.

11. Mark Danner, *The Massacre at El Mozote: A Parable of the Cold War* (New York: Vintage, 1994).

The *Victims* paradigm abides, pitting the power of historical change against the abiding rhythms of everyday life. But of course new details have been added. My speculation about Keith and Allen being related has been confirmed—they were cousins. The Marshall raid was led by a Union guerrilla leader, John Kirk, who was recruiting or seeking refuge in the Laurel Valley. This would have validated Confederate concerns that the amateur Unionism—the intermittent Unionism—of the region might be turning in more organized, professional, and hence more dangerous ways. The massacre sounded an alarm to Confederate officials that the brutality of the war was escalating. Residents of the region became alienated more and more from the Confederate cause. Killing Unionists spawned more Unionism, or at least anti-Confederate feelings.[12] Beyond these points, the story I told in 1981 seems to stand. Scholars have debated the sources of Unionism, but the picture painted here, in which people in or near mountain towns and the larger Southern economy support the Confederacy while those on the fringes of that orbit do not, seems secure if not unchallenged.

That is where scholarship seems to be, but I think that the work is something more than a contribution to Appalachian studies. That is its substance—but the style, the utilization of insights from outside disciplines, still seems to distinguish it. The two thinkers who most shaped the book from outside the historian's discipline were Robert Coles and Robert J. Lifton. Coles told a story of Appalachia that sunk in, especially when it was confirmed by writers from the region like Emma Miles and Cratis Williams. It was a story of a traditional people—traditional even in the 1950s and 1960s when Coles studied them—linked profoundly to their place and customs. They live in the modern world; their lives are shaped by that world, changed by it, but their values—what they are committed to—require holding as tightly as possible to their abiding past. And that condition existed back in the 1860s when a people seen increasingly by outsiders, and by themselves, as separate from the rest of the world encountered the forces of a great transforming, modernizing war. They were swept up in history, which overcame, for a while, their day-to-day lives, their devotion to older ways. The war, in fact, may have contributed

12. John C. Inscoe and Gordon B. McKinney, *The Heart of Confederate Appalachia: Western North Carolina in the Civil War* (Chapel Hill: University of North Carolina Press, 2000), 117–21.

to seeing these people as rough, backwoods, and uncivilized, since they fought guerilla fights against the more organized and disciplined armies of their foes.[13]

Lifton, by exploring "the atrocity producing situation," led me into the minds of the frightened, resentful, perhaps enraged soldiers who marched into a snow-filled valley to face hidden gunmen who bushwhacked the unwary and then ran away. Wars, guerrilla wars especially, produce such moments, and scholars who describe how those moments feel can enrich our understanding and our empathy.

Victims may contribute to the historiography of Southern Appalachian wartime. But I was more interested in trying to understand how an atrocity occurs, in how a general environment can nurture it, how the pressures of war can encourage it, how men can be driven to murder people who are at their mercy. I'm not at all sure that I told the story as well as I hoped to. But I want to believe that storytelling, integrated with views and perspectives from all relevant fields, ought to characterize the historian's work. We ought to try to think like novelists and tell the stories of mankind. Charles Frazier's wonderful novel *Cold Mountain* isn't really about the Civil War; it is a love story and an environmental meditation. But as I think about that war after Frazier gave us *Cold Mountain,* I know more about it now than I did before. The imaginary world he created helps explain what happened in the North Carolina Mountains in the atrocity-producing situation of Civil War. Frazier used a bit of my book in creating his. *Cold Mountain* wasn't around when I wrote *Victims,* but I hope that readers can see something of a novelist's imagination here.[14]

VICTIMS MEETS THE PUBLISHERS

This book tells a story based on, and grounded pretty deeply in, historical documents. It interprets those documents and present them by using techniques and insights from every relevant discipline I could imagine. But it almost didn't see the light of publication. It was

13. Kenneth Noe, "Appalachia's Civil War Generals," *West Virginia History* 50 (1991): 91–108; *Civil War in Appalachia,* ed. Noe and Wilson, xxv.

14. Charles Frazier, *Cold Mountain* (New York: Atlantic Monthly Press, 1997). For a recent call to utilize fiction's empathic styles, see Andrew R. L. Cayton, "Insufficient Woe: Sense and Sensibility in Writing Nineteenth Century History," *Reviews in American History* 31 (September 2003): 331–41.

rejected by presses at the University of North Carolina, the University of Illinois, Louisiana State University, the University of Kansas and the University of Tennessee. The rejection by North Carolina produced one of the most scathing reader's reports that I have ever seen—with due allowance for my personal insecurities. The reader hated everything about the manuscript: research, writing, subject matter; I half expected some remark about the typeface and paper color. The acquiring editor at North Carolina tried to salvage the situation (there was a positive review there too) but couldn't do so. And so he suggested that I send the manuscript to the University of Tennessee Press. They rejected it in what seemed like world-record time. So off I went to the other presses and received their rejections in time.

So, how did Tennessee end up publishing this book? Foundation intervention. I received a Guggenheim Foundation grant to finish up *A People's Contest.* When scholars get those grants, alert presses send recipients notes of congratulations mentioning, not in passing, the hope that, when the time to publish their projects comes, the authors will keep said presses in mind. I got such a letter from Tennessee and huffily replied that they had once precipitously rejected an earlier work of mine. Back came a nice letter, with suitable crow feathers inside, saying that they didn't remember exactly why but how about giving them another chance? Since the manuscript had been sitting neglected for about a year and no one else was clamoring for it I, gracefully, agreed.

Twenty-three years have passed, and I have been delighted with the press's attention and promotion. In that time scholarship on Appalachia in the Civil War has grown and taken fruitful directions. But I still would like to see more explorations of how fiction's styles might inform the search for historical understanding. Sometime in the 1980s, I chaired a panel on new ways of writing history. Three books were the focus of discussion, each with a different device taken from fiction writing but all enlivened by the novelistic sensitivity that style shapes, and informs, substance. David Farber's *Chicago 1968* presented the different stories of the Democratic convention that year as told by Mayor Daley, members of the Mobilization Against the War, and Abby Hoffman's *Yippies* in the dialects common to each, ranging from disciplined rational order to the romantic empathies of kids in the streets. How they spoke molded what they said; style shaped substance. And Farber added to the impact by using different typefaces for each "voice." Eleanor Langer's *Josephine Herbst* so interwove her personal voice with that of Herbst that at times the reader did not know who was speaking—as Langer intended, since the parallels in the lives of the two women were mutually informing. Robert Rosenstone's *Mirror in the Shrine* explored the interactions between his own travels to Japan and the encounters of American travelers centuries before. And with the simple device of putting quotations in italics rather than in quotation marks, he fused past and present, revealing the connections between author and subject. Nothing seemed more appropriate for introducing this panel than to sing—hopefully breaking, in another way, the objective distancing of professional discourse. The song I chose was James Taylor's "Sweet Baby James." I was drawn to the lyric where the cowboy, ostensibly alone, sings out his song "as if maybe someone could hear." The words create an audience, evoke a world beyond what the cowboy objectively sees—but something we now know is there.

In *Victims* I relied on that view to call forth, out of the evidence we have about uncivil war in the North Carolina Mountains, what we can? might? should? believe is there. I believe that all of our imagination, disciplined by a deep respect for fact, needs to be used to understand certain moments in the past when human beings horribly (or happily) discovered what kind of people they are. I don't believe that I took this story to the limit, but in the words of another popular song, I've "gone about as far as I can go." Better writers than me will take up the task, I hope.

Phillip Shaw Paludan
Naomi Lynn Distinguished Chair of Lincoln Studies
University of Illinois, Springfield
February 2004

PREFACE
TO THE
FIRST
EDITION

And as they are Hellenes themselves they will not devastate Hellas, nor will they burn houses, nor ever suppose that the whole population of a city—men, women, and children are equally their enemies, for they know that the guilt of war is always confined to a few persons and that the many are their friends. And for all these reasons they will be unwilling to waste their lands. . . . their enmity to them will only last until the many innocent sufferers have compelled the guilty few to give satisfaction.

PLATO, *The Republic*

In January 1863, in a remote Appalachian valley of North Carolina called Shelton Laurel, thirteen prisoners ranging in age from thirteen to fifty-nine were shot to death. Soldiers recruited from the region, led by two officers from a nearby town, did the actual killing, but in all probability a general who would later be a friend and lieutenant of Robert E. Lee had given the orders that led to the murders. This book is the story of that atrocity.

At least 600,000 men died in the Civil War. Major battles numbered the dead in the thousands; even minor skirmishes killed hundreds. "What I deal in is too vast for malice," Lincoln said, and he was right. Then why study the death of thirteen men? There are several reasons. First, to do so is to encounter the killing, what Whitman called "the real war," at a level with human scale. How can we understand the meaning of this war whose deaths are described in the thousands? Mass death numbs the mind and heart as it numbers its vast toll. Relief from the horror is less possible when we watch old Joe Woods and thirteen-year-old David Shelton plead for life — and then die.

Second, the small scale of this incident requires an investigation of the complexity of historical experience that studies of vast campaigns and huge battles can escape. To look at smaller events, we must explore the lives of specific people — their thoughts and feelings, their families, the neighborhood and community experiences that shaped their reactions to the invasion of their lives by war. The narrower focus can provoke, ironically, a search for a wider range of topics for study, in order to connect social, economic, and political forces with military events. In this case, to bastardize a comment of architect Mies van der Rohe, less is more. Aristotle argued that the historian explores what happened; the small-scale study makes that exploration more subtle, more complex, more in line with history as it is experienced, life as it is lived.

Aristotle further tried to distinguish historians from poets by saying that the poet speaks of the kind of thing that can happen. Northrop Frye clarifies the distinction by saying that historians want to know what happened, poets what happens. Yet in the writing of history the distinction is impossible. Historians want also to know what happens to mankind generally, what historical perspective can contribute to understanding enduring elements in human experience. I have been drawn to study Shelton Laurel because I am concerned with My Lai and the Holocaust, in the tragic capacity that humans have shown throughout history — the capacity to commit atrocity.

A third reason for attention to this subject is that the guerrilla war in the Appalachians has not been extensively studied, and the event itself has been at most a footnote in studies of the conflict. This relative neglect of the mountain warfare is unfortunate because, among other things, it involved thousands of people who may have had their histories profoundly affected by the war. Furthermore, study of this region helps to expand our understanding of how the war tested allegiances and loyalties and what that testing cost in arxiety and anguish. In the mountain war the question of allegiance was not easily resolved in the safety of homes surrounded by sympathetic neighbors, secure from faraway battlefields. An allegiance was worn as a target over the heart, amid armed enemies, and loyalty could attract both dangerous friends and mortal enemies.[1]

All these justifications are part of a larger one, perhaps more personal but not without import for historical study generally. Studying the Shelton Laurel massacre has given me the chance to tie the social history of the Civil War era to a concern about the relationship between the grand events that are the focus of most historical investigation and the daily experiences of ordinary life. Meeting the people of Shelton Laurel in the course of this study has helped me make a valuable distinction between the past and history.

The sense of the past in Shelton Laurel is different from what most historians would consider history. The residents are not particularly concerned about linking their past with the flow of greater events outside their valley. They are only slightly interested in the Civil War generally. The past they are involved in is personal; it focuses on fathers and mothers and grandparents and uncles and aunts and cousins and all their kin, as far back as anyone can remember. They want to know who married whom and had which children and how it was for particular people in moments yesterday and long

---

1. In 1956 Bruce Catton observed that "students of the war almost uniformly (except for some of the Federal generals most directly concerned in the matter) have treated the whole business [of guerrilla warfare] as a colorful, annoying, but largely unimportant side issue." See "Foreword," in Virgil Carrington Jones, *Gray Ghosts and Rebel Raiders* (New York: Holt, 1956), vii–ix. Jones's book is a military study focusing on the dashing exploits of military leaders such as John Mosby. This pattern has been followed in subsequent studies of partisan warfare. The social effect of this warfare has not been the focus of any study that I have found. Three recent studies comment on the impact of the war on mountain society but do not explore the subject: Gordon B. McKinney, *Southern Mountain Republicans, 1865-1900: Politics and the Appalachian Community* (Chapel Hill: Univ. of North Carolina Press, 1978); Henry D. Shapiro, *Appalachia on Our Mind: The Southern Mountains and Mountaineers in the American Consciousness, 1870-1920* (Chapel Hill: Univ. of North Carolina Press, 1978); and Cratis D. Williams, "The Southern Mountaineer in Fact and Fiction" (Ph.D. diss., New York Univ., 1961), rpt. in abridged form in *Appalachian Journal* 3 (1975), 8–61, 100–62, 186–261. The most useful background studies for my work have been John G. Barrett, *Civil War in North Carolina* (Chapel Hill: Univ. of North Carolina Press, 1963), and William D. Cotton, "Appalachian North Carolina" (Ph.D. diss., Univ. of North Carolina, 1954). Also helpful is Charles Faulkner Bryan, "The Civil War in East Tennessee: A Social, Political and Economic Study" (Ph.D. diss., Univ. of Tennessee, 1978).

ago—times that link kin with kin over time, even as they are linked together today in this place. When people in the valley talk about the Civil War, they care little about the conflict of cultures or the breakdown of politics or the wave of modernization. The war to them means the murder of their great-grandfathers and great-uncles and cousins. It means the time when Granny Franklin had to watch soldiers burn down her house and kill her three sons who were hiding there and what she did after the war when one of her brothers murdered one of the soldiers involved.

Yes, of course, that happened in the war, happened because of the war. But the people are not interested in the war as history. They are interested in the past of "Mr. Bud" Shelton who lives across from Glendora's and whose grandpa was one of those murdered in 1863. They do not care that you are a historian who might be able to put such events "in a larger context." They expect historians to get their facts wrong—to make Granny Franklin a Rebel instead of a Unionist ("She'd turn over in her grave if she heard that"). They know what happened, but on the scale of daily life—in the past that they experience and that their dead kin experienced. Essentially they are not a part of history so much as a part of family and kin and generations. They may even resent history. For in the winter of 1863 it ripped into their past and thirteen of their kin were systematically murdered.[2]

Despite this distinction between the past and history, there is a sense in which professional historians have much to learn from the pasts of the Sheltons of the nation. To the extent that we wish to tell the truest possible story about the past, to that extent we must try to recapture the experiences of people who try to escape the forces of history. These forces are too large for individuals; they transcend our control. They sweep in and upset the patterns we have grown used to—the day-to-day way we do things, whose very ordinariness makes those patterns precious. The forces of history have ways of robbing us, of wrenching from us those private things and persons whose comings and goings, whose rhythms, give our lives meaning and protect us and which, despite the recurrent boredom and futil-

2. Interview, April 4, 1977, Mrs. Paul Wallin Shelton and Paula Shelton, Shelton Laurel, N.C.; Glendora Cutchell, "The First Sheltons in America" (mimeographed family history); Manley Wade Wellman, *The Kingdom of Madison* (Chapel Hill: Univ. of North Carolina Press, 1973), 143–44. I am grateful to my colleague Thomas J. Lewin for suggesting this distinction between the past and history.

ity of the mundane, are the signs of the small humanities of ordinary human beings.

It is something like what Finley Peter Dunne's "Mr. Dooley" said — we want to know what a society lived of as well as what it died of. And in this search the little pasts of otherwise unimportant people become crucial, not just in the sense of helping us learn the full story but also as a way of keeping us in touch with our own humanity, of making us aware of those things that we try to shelter from the onslaught of history, those impersonal forces that control us and rush to shatter the living regularities that we long to keep alive. We need to study what it is that keeps us from being victims of history. Shelton Laurel and its people are appealing because, despite history, they seem to have found so many ways to keep on being what they are, keep on knowing who they are and where they came from.[3]

Yet no one can move untouched in the patterns their past has shaped. History hurries near and, unlooked for, is upon us. Then what we are does not shelter, it imprisons. What we are, what we have spent so much time and so much care becoming, compels us to be true to ourselves, to respond our way, our own small, treasured, hard-won way. It can be a way unsuited to history's demands, and it can make us victims, too.

Although the massacre is an interesting and important topic and although its small size adds to the value of studying it, obstacles loom to impede inquiry. Only one of the figures directly involved in the incident left anything approaching a satisfactory documentary record. Because of his association with Lee, because he rose to the rank of general and took the time to write his memoirs, Henry Heth left behind a significant amount of evidence. The record is silent in important places, but it provides a basis for extended analysis. Of the two officers at the scene, Lawrence Allen left only a short memoir prepared by a close associate, and nothing has come down directly from James A. Keith. Readers will therefore perhaps find more than they wish to know about Heth and much less than they are eager to know about Keith and Allen. If it is any consolation, no

3. Finley Peter Dunne, *Observations by Mr. Dooley* (New York: R.H. Russell, 1902), 271. I am reminded of an observation by John Passmore in *The Perfectability of Man* (London: Duckworth, 1970); he points out the dangers of forgetting the little loves that give us our humanity in the service of the larger loves that generate great historical movements.

one feels this frustration more than myself — and mine has lasted for years. But, telling the fullest story possible on the basis of existing evidence has been an obligation I have felt, and so Heth receives here a share of attention disproportionate to his role in the killings.

Yet in another sense Heth deserves attention. To the extent that this study of a nineteenth-century atrocity informs us about atrocity generally, far more people play roles such as Heth played than are on the scene as murderers. More people tolerate, condone, permit than actually execute the deed. There are far many more "attendant lords" than Lord Hamlets. Outrage at those who pull the triggers should not allow us to ignore the roles played by others who are implicated. In fact, these latter may be worth more attention. Those who kill are potentially excusable, for they often act in circumstances where they may not see alternatives. Those who order, encourage, or allow the killing do so where the dangers are less, where alternatives may be considered. There is more for them to explain and more to be explained about them.

My interest in this incident, combined with the scarcity of pertinent materials, has provoked a search not just for documents but also for angles of vision that might expand my understanding. Some of the approaches I have taken go up to and perhaps beyond the boundaries of traditional historical research. In addition to relying on letters and travel accounts, official reports and manuscript censuses describing Appalachian North Carolina, I have used interviews with current residents and studies by sociologists and anthropologists of the twentieth-century mountain region. In addition to asking what happened, I have sought to understand and apply generalizations drawn from the sociology of communities and from studies of modernization as avenues for exploring why it happened. I have also ventured into psychological studies of soldiers in Vietnam and elsewhere in seeking to understand the dynamics of the atrocity-producing situation.

This use of modern social science literature raises the question of whether insights drawn from such sources properly can be applied to events of a past century. For two major reasons I believe that they can. As the first chapter shows, Shelton Laurel belongs to a part of the United States where old ways are tenaciously held. The past is very present in the Appalachian highlands. Secondly, the incident under study is one of a type not confined to one period of history. It involves primary emotions that are less a part of a certain moment in history and more a part of the human personality. This is not to say that historical circumstances do not play a major role in helping to create a situation; this book is a study of how they in fact do so. It is only to insist that at the time in which a decision is made to commit a massacre, in an environment in which someone permits it to happen, fears and anxieties that exist throughout history emerge to unleash the tragedy. It has seemed to me that psychologists who studied the Vietnam war have significant things to say about such moments.

My search for angles of vision on this incident has led me beyond modern social science and into the nature of historical writing itself. I have sought to expand understanding of this incident and tried to capture the incident's complexity, by writing about it in a style that calls forth the reader's emotional resources as an aid to understanding. I am trying to appeal to informed hearts as well as minds. I want the reader to empathize with both the victims and the killers, to share the sense of what it was like to live in that place and commit that act. I want the reader not just to gain an understanding of how the act happened and why, but to experience what it felt like to have it happen. These two types of insight will, I believe, mutually inform each other. Readers of serious novels will find no surprise in this assertion.[4]

I respect detached objective observation. I am trying to engage in it. I also am wary of its capacity for vivisection as well as analysis. I do not believe that we can fully understand the experiences of people if we act only as detached analysts, if we neglect or repress our desire to feel the past as well as to analyze it. We do not really have to choose between the two, and I have not attempted to do so in this book. I have tried to use a writing style that will enlarge understanding, to use such detached observation as a historian is capable of to analyze that experience, and to call upon available insights from

4. See J.H. Hexter, *The History Primer* (New York: Basic Books, 1971) for the most recent argument in favor of the study of history as an empathetic understanding of the past. For a recent collection of essays on the nature of historical narrative, see Robert H. Canary and Henry Kozicki, eds., *The Writing of History: Literary Form and Historical Understanding* (Madison: Univ. of Wisconsin Press, 1978).

other disciplines to enlarge understanding. I have tried to do what I think all historians try to do: use every available resource to describe what happened in the past and to convey what they believe is important to remember about it.

PSP
Lawrence Kansas
December 1980

ACKNOWLEDGMENTS

Every work of scholarship is a community effort. The work of pred-
ecessors establishes insights and points to new directions. Friends
and colleagues nourish the inquiry with questions and suggestions
and most of all by caring about what an author is trying to do. Loved
ones sustain the effort by caring about the author, whatever he tries
to do. Libraries and librarians facilitate research by involvement in
the project that usually goes far beyond simply handing over materials. Funding agencies give an author both the money to travel to
his sources and the precious, indispensable time to write and think.
I thank them all for what they do every day for all of us, but I have
more specific debts to acknowledge.

I thank the American Council of Learned Societies and the Harvard Law School Liberal Arts Fellowship Program for providing
the legal training that helped me understand the legal issues at stake
here. Later the ACLS provided a semester in which I could write
and think about small communities and war. The American Philo-
sophical Society made possible a trip to the South, and the Hunting-
ton Library gave me a place to work and the incomparable assistance of its staff of readers and librarians. The University of Kansas

General Research Fund helped make summers a time for research and writing.

My colleagues at the University of Kansas involved themselves in this effort and educated me in the process. Rita G. Napier, in countless conversations on every subject, but mostly on Indians and communities, has helped me understand these subjects. N. Ray Hiner gave guidance in psychohistory. David Katzman and John Clark pointed the paths in community study. Thomas Lewin helped in thinking about oral evidence, and Clifford Griffin again challenged me to think about what writing history means. Donald McCoy was constant in his encouragement and generous in his time and friendship. John Lomax gave invaluable research assistance. Former colleague Charles Warner helped at the beginning of the project, and the late Richard Reinitz of Hobart and William Smith colleges kept me going toward the end with his lovely combination of critical insight and personal friendship. Harold Hyman has continued to be an interested and insightful mentor. The suggestions made by Eric Foner and Stephen Oates as readers of this manuscript for the University of Tennessee Press have improved it greatly. Ron Eller of Mars Hill College also made the book a better one.

Special acknowledgments go to William Shelton, Jr., of Columbus, Ohio, whose correspondence was filled with information and encouragement. Mrs. Paul Wallin Shelton of Shelton Laurel gave me her time, hospitality, and much information about her family and its history, as did her daughter Paula. Glendora Cutchell was also kind and helpful in providing material about the valley. Although some of the Sheltons pictured in this book were not always admirable, the people I met in Shelton Laurel were uniformly helpful and kind and very well informed on their region's history. Without their help there are many things I would never have understood.

Finally, as this book is about how ordinary people encounter the forces of history, my family has contributed to it immeasurably. Grandfathers and grandmothers, aunts and uncles, mother and father, wife and children, as they lived and live from day to day have inescapably called forth more than scholarly questions about this encounter. By their concern for me, these people have made this book possible, but they have also become part of the subject itself. I think I am as grateful for the one as for the other.

VICTIMS A TRUE STORY OF THE CIVIL WAR

1

THE PLACE

Look now in the faces of those that
you love and remember
That you are not thinking of death.

JULIAN SYMONS, "Pub"

For almost three generations the valley had sustained and sheltered them. As the valley wound its way between the ancient rounded mountaintops, it sometimes spread out as wide as three-quarters of a mile, and there was room to grow corn, beans, and sweet potatoes. Deer, bears, possums, and squirrels shared the place and provided meat for the table. The Shelton Laurel Creek traced its path through the valley, providing water and fish. And there was usually forage enough to fatten the wild pigs that ran loose until winter killing time. But the valley was not a garden. It gave what it had of these resources only after hard work, and although they were not frequent, there were hungry times. Still, the place gave sustenance, and that guaranteed, there were few reasons to leave and more to stay.

As it gave them food, the place also protected them. Where their creek joined the Laurel River the pass was narrow and stayed that way; steep mountainsides followed the creek's crooked meanderings for about a mile. Tangled laurel bushes crowded around wild locust trees, sourwoods, oaks, chestnuts, tulip poplars, and pines. Men

3

with rifles could be deadly defenders in such terrain. Other entrances to the valley were almost as difficult; all staggered through twisted valleys and practically impenetrable vegetation. In Madison County, North Carolina, where the Appalachians crested along the Tennessee line, nature had prepared her defenses well. Only the most determined of forces could invade the place. And yet the invasion came, and death came with it.

Governor Zebulon Vance was from those North Carolina mountains. He might have expected something like this to happen. He knew the fierce independence of the mountaineers and knew that they could be brutal if it came to a fight. He knew also that the war raging in the mountains in that winter of 1862–63 swirled with the intense hatred that only guerrilla warfare can spawn. Perhaps he also knew that tradition had marked the place with blood. White settlers had wrenched it from the Cherokees in a struggle in which the massacres by one side were answered with massacres by the other. The Indians had prayed there to their god of the hunt: "Oh great Kanati, I come where you repose. Let your bosom be covered with bloodstained leaves."[1]

At first it was not clear exactly what had happened. Reports of the murder came in slowly. Vance's long-time friend A.S. Merrimon first broke the news in late January 1863 of what had happened in Shelton Laurel. "I learn that a number of *prisoners* were *shot* without any trial or hearing whatever. I hope it is not true, but if so, the parties guilty of so dark a deed should be punished. Humanity revolts at such a crime."[2] Vance had feared that the mountain warfare would spawn brutality, but an immense burden of work was falling on him as the new year began, and he apparently misunderstood what Merrimon told him. "I was . . . sorry to learn this morning," he wrote to an officer near the scene, "that Colonel Lawrence Allen had hanged several of the captured prisoners." Confused or not, he wanted to know more of what happened. By the sixteenth of February, Merrimon could tell him: "I have no knowledge of my own touching the shooting. . . . I have learned, however, from a most

1. Wilma Dykeman, *The French Broad* (1955; rpt. 1965, Knoxville: Univ. of Tennessee Press), 41.
2. Merrimon to Vance, Jan. 31, 1863, Governors Papers, North Carolina State Archives, Raleigh, N.C. Merrimon's italics.

reliable source that thirteen of them were killed; that some of them were not taken in arms but at their homes; that all the men shot . . . were prisoners at the time they were shot; that they were taken off to a secluded cove or gorge in the mountains and then made to kneel down and were thus shot. One man was badly and mortally shot in the bowels, and while he was writhing in agony and praying to God for mercy a soldier mercilessly and brutally shot him in the head with his pistol. Several women were whipped; this I learned from someone who got his information from some of the guilty parties. I learn that all this was done by order of Lieut. Col. James A. Keith."[3]

Within a week Merrimon had the names of the victims and the ages for some of them: Elison King; Joe Woods; Will Shelton, age twenty; Halen Moore, age twenty-five or thirty; Wade Moore, age twenty or twenty-five; Old Jim Shelton, age fifty-six; James Shelton, Jr., age seventeen; James Metcalf, age forty; Stob Rob Shelton; David Shelton (brother of Stob Rod); Jasper Chandler, age fifteen or sixteen; and David Shelton, age thirteen. Although Merrimon's understanding was limited, the overall picture was clear. The Civil War had come to a remote mountain valley called Shelton Laurel.

It had come ripping into the fabric of a life whose rhythms were seldom interrupted. The ordinary pattern of life in Shelton Laurel was set by nature, by the seasons, and by the ages of a human life — birth, childhood, marriage, maturity, old age, and death — by the growing of crops and the varying habits of hunting and fishing, cooking, mending, and weaving. These rhythms marked the flow of life in the mountains, much as they did throughout most of the United States. Over two-thirds of the people in 1860 were rural, sensitive to forces they could not control: nature or God determining death, survival, prosperity. Their ties to their homes were strong, making concrete their encounters with these forces, linking death with the nearby graves of their loved ones, prosperity or survival with the harvests from fields once fenced or planted by their parents. Over three-fourths of the native population in the nineteenth century lived in the state they were born in.

Other forces were also loose in this society. Americans were becoming a people increasingly eager to control their destinies, dissat-

3. Merrimon to Vance, Feb. 16, 1863; Vance to Davis, Feb. 2, 1863, *Official Record of the War of the Rebellion,* ser. 1, vol. 18, 867, 881 (hereafter cited as *OR*).

isfied with being subject to external forces. They did what they could to take advantage of soil, water, and wildlife, raping the land and its resources sometimes consciously, sometimes thoughtlessly. Afloat on a natural tide they could not stop, they still struggled to control the land and to take advantage of it and of each other. Although the needs of the harvest were compelling, the sense of man intertwined with the land did not take deep root. Most American farmers were distinguished by the fact that to them the land was real estate, something to be marketed, to be speculated on. Farmers bought land as much to sell to later buyers as to farm on. Often these sellers would take their profit and move on to another place. "Men in motion" and "people on the move"—these were the terms applied to Americans.[4]

Nevertheless, Americans were a people connected to the soil. When they were at rest, as even the most mobile of them were for most of their lives, they marched to a cadence set not by the drum or the hum of the machine, but by place, and the time of year, and techniques and habits followed for generations.

Like most Americans in 1860, the people of Shelton Laurel were rural people. They differed in carrying the rural rhythm to its extreme. Like thousands of people in hundreds of mountain valleys up and down the Appalachians, they were linked intimately with place as well as with nature. People did not just reside in Shelton Laurel; they were a part of it. They did not sell the land to strangers. They did not speculate on it. They kept the land and passed it on to their descendants, who raised their children on it and gave the land to the children who had grown up on it. And the children stayed and raised their children within Shelton Laurel, until the place and the people were almost one.

Before the mid-nineteenth century this had not been the case.

4. *Statistical History of the United States* (Stamford, Conn., n.d.), 14, 41; Peter Knights and Stephen Thernstrom, "Men in Motion: Some Data and Speculations about Urban Population Mobility," in *Anonymous Americans,* ed. Tamara Haraven (Englewood Cliffs, N.J.: Prentice-Hall, 1971), 17–47. Historians have focused their attention on statistics revealing mobility and thereby have undervalued the stability of the majority of the population. It should be noted that the places for which most studies of geographic mobility have been made are places where most mobility is likely to exist: the frontier and the cities. See the table of these studies in Stephen Thernstrom, *The Other Bostonians* (Cambridge: Harvard Univ. Press, 1975), 226.

When the mountain highlands were originally settled, they were no more isolated than any other frontier region, and the people were not distinguished from other frontiersmen and borderers. The land was not uniquely noted for poverty, violence, or the ignorance of its residents. Indeed, observers often remarked on the superiority of mountain people in wealth, industry, and intelligence.

Although time would work changes on people's view of mountain life, the wealthy, well-educated, industrious mountaineer would never disappear from the region. A range of social and economic possibilities existed in the highlands. There were throughout history large, extensively cultivated farms close to main roads and market centers. The prosperous farmers who lived there participated in the movement of people and goods in and out of the mountains. While it was more difficult for them to travel than it was for people in the piedmont and tidewater sections of the South, they still could and did participate in the world outside the mountains.

Close by in the towns and villages were men equally in touch with outside currents. Their focus was on making their towns prosperous and important in their neighborhood or region. Such ambition did not remove their attachment to the mountain region; rather, it gave this feeling a cosmopolitan quality. The people might love the wilderness around them and believe their place superior to the rest of the world, but their hopes for themselves and their place emphasized progress, growth, and change.

The important people in the mountain region were often wealthy farmers who divided their time between cultivating the land and providing the professional and economic services needed in the trade centers and towns. These men were often the doctors, the lawyers, the ministers, and the store owners, as well as the sheriffs, the judges, and other town officials. The towns also attracted laborers and clerks to do heavy and menial tasks, and larger landowners could rent their land to tenants. What distinguished these people from other mountaineers such as those in Shelton Laurel was their contact with the larger world, either in actual trade or in aspirations. The towns touched the outside world by being places where traders gathered, travelers stopped, and courts met. They also served as administrative centers exercising the power of law over the more isolated highlanders as well as the local population. As the southern economy grew in the 1840s, '50s, and '60s, these places took on additional life.[5]

Yet as mountain towns and their neighborhoods developed, another phenomenon was taking place as well. Rural mountaineers were becoming more isolated from the outside world, and it was these people who came to be predominantly identified as the true people of the mountains. By the 1840s and 1850s the isolation of the southern mountaineers was becoming apparent to outsiders as well as to the people themselves. The pattern of future decades was becoming set. Visitors, while still commenting on occasional signs of wealth and industry, began to note large families competing for limited land, increasing poverty and ignorance, and curious customs of a quaint people. The visitors reported conversations in which the mountaineers showed striking ignorance of the world outside (New York was thought to be somewhere near Texas) and amazement over the fact that New Yorkers did not know one another as well as the people in mountain valleys did. By the 1870s and '80s observers were speaking of "our contemporary ancestors" and seeking ways to bring respectable Christianity, the work ethic, and education to the gaunt and violent "hillbillys" and "moonshiners."[6]

The settlement of the Shelton Laurel valley epitomized this pattern. The Sheltons were the first white people to arrive. Although the family can trace its ancestry to English royalty, the Sheltons who first came to the Laurel valley were hardly recognizable as nobility. In the early 1790s, just after the land was taken from the Cherokees, two brothers named David and Martin Shelton came to the place from Virginia. Martin chose to live in the burned-out insides of a

---

5. Cratis Williams, "The Southern Mountaineer in Fact and Fiction," *Appalachian Journal* 3 (1975), 22–24; Harry Schwartzweller, James S. Brown, and J.J. Mangalam, *Mountain Families in Transition* (University Park: Penn State Univ. Press, 1971), 3–6; Manuscript Census of the United States, Madison County, N.C., 1860; Guion Griffis Johnson, *Ante-Bellum North Carolina: A Social History* (Chapel Hill: Univ. of North Carolina Press, 1937), 620–27. Although published too late to be fully incorporated into my research, the recent article by Ronald Eller, "Land and Family: An Historical View of Preindustrial Appalachia," *Appalachian Journal* 6 (Winter 1979), 83–109, sustains most of the discussion here.

6. Williams, "Southern Mountaineer in Fact and Fiction," 18–25, 42–61; Frederick Law Olmsted, *A Journey in the Back Country* (New York: Mason Bros., 1863), 221–82; "R," "A Week in the Great Smoky Mountains," *Southern Literary Messenger,* Aug. 1860, 119–30; Shapiro, *Appalachia on Our Mind,* passim; McKinney, *Southern Mountain Republicans,* 3–11.

hollow tree. David sought more human surroundings, but both brothers were living in the wilderness when the boundary commissioners came through in 1799. The area remained so wild that it was not until 1815 that anyone could record their holdings. When they could, the Shelton brothers were the first to do so, staking their claim to an area on "Lorrel Creek."

The Sheltons, and people like them, endured in that place. In 1796 there were forty-four different names on a land survey list for the mountain counties of what was to be Buncombe, Madison, Transylvania, Henderson, and part of Haywood counties. By 1921 thirty-four of those names remained. In 1826, when a few new families moved into the Shelton Laurel region, they found the Sheltons, the Franklins, the Rices, and the Cutchells already in residence. In April of 1977, when I visited Shelton Laurel, I stopped at Glendora Cutchell's store, got directions to Paul Shelton's house, and talked throughout a rainy afternoon to Mrs. Shelton about her family and about the Rices and the Franklins still living there. The people of the Shelton Laurel abide.[7]

It is not just a case of people remaining in one place; it is of people and their place being entwined. And this abiding attachment suggests that the ideas and culture of past generations still hold sway in modern times, that the insights of twentieth-century observers can illuminate the world of a century ago. In the 1960s Robert Coles lived in a mountain valley for several months and observed the bonding of people and place. One afternoon he was visiting a family he knew well, and the mother, after nursing her baby, brought him out into the sun. She "put the child down on the ground, and gently fondled him, and moved him a bit with her feet, which were not usually covered with shoes or socks. The child did not cry. The mother seemed to have almost exquisite control of her toes. It all seemed very nice, but I really had no idea what [she] really had in mind until she leaned over and spoke very gravely to her child: 'This is your land and it's time you started getting to know it.'"[8]

7. John C. Campbell, *The Southern Highlander and His Homeland* (New York: Russell Sage, 1921), 64–67; Manley Wade Wellman, *The Kingdom of Madison*, 63, 143–44, 195–96; Glendora Cutchell, "The First Sheltons in America"; interview with Mrs. Paul Wallin Shelton, Shelton Laurel, N.C., April 4, 1977.
8. Robert Coles, *Migrants, Sharecroppers, Mountaineers*, (Boston: Little, Brown, 1971), 203–204; Emma Bell Miles, *The Spirit of the Mountains* (1905; rpt. 1975, Knoxville: Univ. of Tennessee Press), 17–19.

Placed on the ground, the children crawled and rolled and lay on it. They explored and felt and smelled and caressed it, and they stumbled and bruised themselves and sometimes, when they were very young, they got lost. But in the course of it all they became part of the place and loved it profoundly. It is a love that grew, as mountain woman Emma Bell Miles recalled in 1905, "from a babyhood when the thrill of clean wet sand was good to little feet; when 'froghouses' were built, and little tracks were printed in rows all over the shore of the creek; when the beginnings of aesthetic feeling found expression in necklaces of scarlet haws and headdresses pinned and braided together of oak leaves, cardinal flowers and fern; when beargrass in spring, 'sarvices,' and berries in summer and muscadines in autumn were first sought after and prized most for the 'wild flavor,' the peculiar tang of the woods which they contain."[9]

Of course, the inroads of the modern world brought changes. Good roads, radio, television, increasing literacy, all twentieth-century invaders, have ways of sweeping over the most isolated people and pushing them into the modern world. But mountaineers do not go gently into the new age. They know they pay an enormous price — that the traditions of centuries are in peril when the invader comes. One of the most soul-wrenching experiences for them comes when they must leave to find work. Then they confront the real meaning of what they are about to lose, and it is the land that they miss the most — their place. Faced with this loss, they embrace it in their thoughts with profound tenderness. Even though life is hard, and sometimes there may be almost nothing to eat, and the children get sick and die, and a woman can lose all her teeth before she is thirty, still, when they have to leave: "If I don't have to go, maybe it'll be my sons. They'll be the ones to cry and not me. They'll be looking ahead, I know. But it'll be a shame for us to leave, my family; it's a shame when you leave the only thing you've known, your land — and remember, it's the land that's seen you trying and that's tried back, tried to give you all it could."[10]

9. Miles, *Spirit of the Mountains,* 17-18.
10. Coles, *Migrants, Sharecroppers, Mountaineers,* 23-24; John B. Stephenson, *Shiloh: A Mountain Community* (Lexington: Univ. of Kentucky Press, 1968), 21-22. In 1905 Emma Bell Miles noted, "Occasionally a whole starved-out family will emigrate westward, and, having settled, will spend years in simply waiting for a chance to sell out and move back again. All alike cling to the ungracious acres they

This profound intermingling of people and land goes deep into the past. It is perhaps the most enduring of the mountaineers' characteristics. Bonded with the land, embraced with it, the mountaineers have not only seen the movement of the seasons, they have also come to know that the flow of seasons is a cycle that endures, that links past and present with the future and makes the present inextricably the past because there is so little to distinguish today from yesterday or tomorrow. Even twentieth-century observers have called the mountaineers "yesterday's people." At a time when the modern world intruded from a hundred directions, they held it at bay far better than most Americans. Their isolation, their stability, their relationship with their land keep the past present.[11]

"Every phase of the mountaineer's life connects in some way with tradition currently received," wrote Emma Miles. "Castaways," a visitor called them ten years later. Like people living "on some unknown island . . . untroubled by the growth of civilization . . . customs and ideas unaltered from the time of their fathers . . . mountain folks still live in the Eighteenth Century." Englishman Cecil Sharp sought authentic eighteenth-century English folk music and came to the Laurel country in the early 1900s. There he found not just old people but young as well who could sing the songs he sought, and in the mountains in and near Shelton Laurel he collected more than 350 of these songs and ballads.[12]

Even in our own time observers are struck by the power of the past in the lives of these people. Social science teams calculate and quantify, apply modern analytical frameworks to mountain communities, and conclude, "Traditionalism lay back of every aspect of [this community's] culture, sanctioning and accounting for the behavior, attitudes and valued ideals of the . . . people. Most of the beliefs and practices in these mountain neighborhoods were handed down relatively intact from one generation to another, and because

have so patiently and hardly won, because of the wild world that lies outside their puny fences, because of the dream vistas, blue and violet, that lead their eyes afar among the hills." Miles, *Spirit of the Mountains,* 18–19.

11. Jack E. Weller, *Yesterday's People. Life in Contemporary Appalachia* (Lexington: Univ. of Kentucky Press, 1965).

12. Olive Dame Campbell and Cecil J. Sharp, *English Folk Songs from the Southern Appalachians* (New York: Putnam, 1917); Horace Kephart, *Our Southern Highlanders* (1922; rpt. 1976, Knoxville: Univ. of Tennessee Press, 1976), 17; Miles, *Spirit of the Mountains,* 98.

they were the beliefs and practices of one's fathers and forefathers they were deemed right, they were prescriptions to be followed." Robert Coles captured the feeling of this tradition in two revealing incidents. After attending a funeral, Coles and a mountaineer got to talking about what death means and the man told him, "When I was a boy I recall my people burying their old people right near where we lived. We had a little graveyard and we used to know all our dead people pretty well. You know, we'd play near their graves and go ask our mother or daddy who this one was and what he did and like that."

Coles also asked eight-year-old "Billy Potter" to draw a picture of himself in the future. It is a request that children in other places, rich and poor, respond to eagerly, yet this child said he could not do it. Coles explains: "Billy knows exactly where he is and where he will most likely be (if he has anything to say about it) and he also knows why his future seems so assured, so concretely before him, so definite. He knows that the Potters have been in the creek for generations — and that it was no small job in the first place to get there, to dig in and last and last and last over the decades which have now become centuries. He knows that ravines take an immeasurable length of time to come about and he sees himself and his family and his kin and his friends as also part of something well nigh everlasting, something that continues, goes on, stays *there,* however hard and difficult and miserably unfair 'life' can get to be."[13]

Modern residents of Shelton Laurel, young and old, link past and present, too. Within a mile of one another, there are at least three people who actively keep the past alive by studying about and writing down their antiquities. Glendora Cutchell has mimeographed four or five histories of different parts of the Shelton past — each history two to three pages long. These are kept on the counter of her combination home, store, and gas station. "Mr. Bud" Shelton reportedly has 400 pages of family history material. Mrs. Paul Wallin Shelton showed me a large looseleaf notebook of some 400 pages and a three-by-four-foot genealogical chart she has prepared. Her daughter, Paula, sat with us and contributed her own information about the history of the family. In 1968 "Mr. Bud" and about half a

---

13. Coles, *Migrants, Sharecroppers, Mountaineers,* 241, 358; Schwartzweller, Brown, and Mangalam, *Mountain Families in Transition,* 67.

dozen other Shelton kinsmen set up two small granite stones to mark the place where the victims of the Civil War murders were buried. They seem not to have done this for the benefit of tourists, because the stones are on a hillside away from even the sporadic traffic on the nearby road. No signs point out the spot, but the Sheltons and their people know where it is.[14]

Throughout the nineteenth century and well into the twentieth, family life maintained the pattern of mountain experience as it did for the larger world. In that family life the men were the masters. From the first days of life a boy learned that he was "the favored lord of all he survey[ed]." At dinner he sat with the men while the women served. He went off into the woods to fish and hunt while the women stayed home and cared for the place. He was the one whose rules were obeyed, and he was the one who went to town when someone had to go. He was the one whom the wider world might touch and corrupt—the one who took to drinking and let his wife and family take the consequences. He was the independent decision maker, and no one outdid the mountaineer in his individualism.[15]

In a society where there were no slaves, it was the woman who provided the nurture, who prepared the home from which the man moved and lived his life and to which he returned. Of course, he was the provider, and providing was no small task on land that had to be cleared and plowed and tended to give even an adequate return. The man had to bring back food for the table, or the family did not eat. Perhaps it was his responsibility and his opportunity to meet the outside world that made him the ruler of his home.[16]

Although men gave the orders, when there were orders to be given, the home was not truly theirs. The men entered the house, wrote Emma Miles, "to eat and sleep, but their life is outdoors, foot-loose in the new forest or on the farm that renews itself crop by crop. His is the high daring and merciless recklessness of youth and the characteristic grim humor of the American, these though he live to be a hundred. Heartily then he conquers his chosen bit of wilder-

14. Interview, Mrs. Paul Wallin Shelton, April 4, 1977; Leon M. Siler, "My Lai Controversy Recalls 1863 Tragedy on the Shelton Laurel," *The State,* Feb. 1, 1970, 9–10.

15. Campbell, *Southern Highlander,* 90–93, 124–25; Weller, *Yesterday's People,* 49; Miles, *Spirit of the Mountains,* 36–70.

16. Miles, *Spirit of the Mountains,* 64–69.

ness and heartily begets and rules his tribe, fighting and praying alike fearlessly and exultantly. . . . For him is the excitement of fighting and journeying, trading, drinking and hunting, of wild rides and nights of danger."[17]

While the men might soar, the women waited and endured. They were the ones who spent nights anxiously watching the sick or waiting for the men to return, perhaps with and perhaps without the food the family needed. Whereas the men were a part of what Miles called "the young nation," the women belonged "to the race, to the *old* people." A mountain woman was old "in toil, sorrow, childbearing, loneliness and pitiful want." She lived in a house nearly always old and "thronged with the memories of other lives." Parents, grandparents, long-dead kin had woven the rug, stitched the quilts, hinged the doors, crafted the shingles and nailed them to the roof, built the house itself. She knew the stories of everything in the place, of people who had lived and suffered and sometimes been happy there, of children who had lived for a short time and then died. And she came to know "that nothing can happen which has not happened before; that whatever she may be called upon to endure . . . others have undergone its like over and over again."[18]

Men and women grew gradually into their roles. Girls slowly took up as many of the household chores as they could handle. Staying at home in a place that basically belonged to the women firmly taught them a woman's place and her duties. Boyhood and manhood fused slowly, too. Boys joined their fathers, brothers, and kin in hunting and farming as soon as they were physically able. They copied the older men as best they could, trying, of course, to grow up as fast as possible, but they kept on being children too. Emma Miles recalled a conversation with a mountain mother whose seven-year-old son worked hard at acting like his father but still was a child when he forgot himself.

"Does he ever want you to rock him to sleep?" Miles asked.

"Oh, when he's sick or tired he's right glad to be my little boy for a while. . . . But he's always a growed up man 'in he wakes up in the morning."[19]

When he was about ten, a boy learned to shoot a gun and went

17. Ibid.
18. Ibid.
19. Ibid., 16.

hunting with the men from time to time. To some extent he was a man then, but not in all things. He lived in his parents' home, was subject to the will of his father or mother, continued to be seen as one of the children. As his responsibility for work grew, he moved more into manhood. And sometime, usually around seventeen to nineteen, the 1860 and 1870 censuses reveal, a boy set out for himself, took over as head of a household, got his own land, became a father.[20]

A boy's movement toward maturity took place in a context of powerful kinship ties, of shared child-rearing tasks, and the many family members were different models for a boy to copy. Older children cared for younger ones and were themselves looked after by those still older. Kin were all around, and there was much mutual caring and responsibility. And if someone died or was killed, the whole group would feel the loss, knowing that a person who had been an abiding part of their lives was gone. If a boy of thirteen were killed, then death had come to someone just learning to be a man, not yet forgetting what it was like to be a child. It had taken someone who had been cared for by older brothers and cousins and uncles, as well as parents. They would all remember him as a little boy trying to be a man. Younger children would recall someone who played with them like a child but who had been able to show them the way to growing up themselves.[21]

For all their differences, men and women were alike in sharing the traditions and necessities of the place. And they were alike in a profound individualism, a quality practically inescapable, given the valley's isolation, but one that could produce a narrowmindedness matched with ignorance. Because mountaineers were so often alone, because the pattern of their lives was so regular, and because their ways of doing things, of behaving, were so well established, self-assurance was their hallmark. A mountaineer tended to know exactly who he was and where he fit in the scheme of things, even

20. Manuscript Census, Madison County, N.C., 1860. On the question of differences between childhood and maturity in the nineteenth century, see Joseph F. Kett, *Rites of Passage* (New York: Basic Books, 1977) 133–43; John Modell et al., "Social Changes and Transition to Adulthood," *Journal of Family History* 1 (Autumn 1976), 7–32.

21. Coles, *Migrants, Sharecroppers, Mountaineers,* 499–502; Miles, *Spirit of the Mountains,* 14; Weller, *Yesterday's People,* 61–64, 69–70; Eller, "Land and Family," 99–102.

though what he was was limited by his physical and intellectual isolation. This limited viewpoint, because it was *his,* was frequently exalted into truth. He did what was right, and it was right because he did it.

Sometimes what he did gained glory and admiration outside the mountains as well as within them. Sometimes he made his mark on larger historical events. People whose traditions included the Regulators, the Mecklenburg Declaration of Independence, and the foundation of the state of Franklin; who encouraged the growth of religious freedom in North Carolina; and who had successfully defied Hamilton's whiskey regulations even as Pennsylvanians were being squashed, harbored not just self-will but pride in what they were. If what they were might often be called ignorant and primitive by outsiders—well, let the outsiders match the mountaineers' history.[22]

Isolation and individualism might thus foster pride and devotion to heritage. But it also nurtured a primitive and potentially dangerous emotionalism. Although their emotionalism could provide release from the pains of life, it could also erupt in a violence linked with self-righteousness. Mountain religion reveals both characteristics. It grew intertwined with the circumstances of the place—from an environment where death was always near, nature was frequently awesome, and man was often the victim of both these forces. What the people needed from God, from somewhere, was a way to explain the unexplainable. More than that, they needed a way to transcend for a time their helplessness, a way to stand not outside these forces but somehow within them.

To Emma Miles, courage seemed to be "the keynote of our whole system of religious thought, the fatalism of this free folk is unlike anything of the Far East; dark and mystical though it be through much brooding over the problems of evil, it is lighted with flashes of the spirit of the Vikings. A man born and bred in a vast wild land nearly always becomes a fatalist. He learns to see Nature not as a thing of fields and brooks, friendly to man and docile beneath his hand, but as a world of depths and heights and distances illimitable, of which he is but a tiny part. He feels himself carried in a sweep of forces too vast for comprehension, forces variously at war, out of

22. Campbell, *Southern Highlander,* 90-95, 126, 159-65; 260.

which are the issues of life and earth, but in which the Order, the Right, must ultimately prevail. This is the beginning of his faith; from thence is his courage and his independence. Inevitably he comes to feel with a sort of proud humility that he has no part or lot in the control of the universe save as he allies himself, by prayer and obedience, with the Order that rules."[23]

How could one take part in things so much larger than man? Not by theology, not by analyzing the scriptures, though the mountaineers could split doctrinal hairs and liked to discuss religion. No, the way to link man and the universe was to become like a little child. As one mountain preacher put it, "I thank Thee, Oh Father, because Thou has hid these things from the wise and prudent and has revealed them unto babes."[24]

When the mountaineers went to church, they sought two things. The first was a community with their fellows, a social gathering where the women especially could exchange gossip and mutual caring and where the young could court and discover someone to care about. This social aspect reflected, at times, a huddling together of isolated people subject to forces they could not control. Secondly, these people sought a direct encounter with the Spirit. They sang hymns that ranged from simple stories of how Jesus's family sang and prayed, to songs celebrating the awesome power of the Lord, to hymns emphasizing the uncertainty of life and the certainty of death and judgment: "Oh ye young, ye gay, ye proud. You must die and wear the shroud. Eternity, eternity. Then you'll cry. I want to be, happy in Eternity." There were the hymns that constantly repeated phrases and words and rhythms, hymns that Emma Miles likened to "the monotonous beating of the West Indians' [drum] that incites their savage minds to frenzy." There were "oddly changing keys . . . endings that leave the ear in expectation of something to follow . . . quavers and falsettos (these) become in recurrence a haunting hint of the spiritual world; neither beneficent nor maleficent, neither devil nor angel, but something—something not to be understood, yet certainly apprehended. It is to the singer as if he stood with a sorcerer's circle crowded upon by an invisible throng."[25]

23. Miles, *Spirit of the Mountains,* 140.
24. Campbell, *Southern Highlander,* 179.
25. Miles, *Spirit of the Mountains,* 150–53; Campbell and Sharp, "Introduction," in *English Folk Songs*; "R," "A Week in the Great Smoky Mountains," 124.

It was not just the singing that stirred them. Gathered together at revival times especially, in a small church building surrounded by mountains and trees and wilderness that dwarfed the place, flickering pine torches dimly lighting the room, the people rocked back and forth to the songs and the prayers, and when sitting became too much for them, they would leap into the air, speak in tongues, shout, scream, sob. Visitors mocked these "noisy declamations in unnatural tones, accompanied by violent physical exercises and manifest emotional excitement [which] in too many cases took the place of intelligent exposition of the truth made vital by the indwelling power of the Spirit." But to the mountaineer these meetings were his encounter with the Spirit at a level of vitality that mere "intelligent exposition" could never approach.[26]

Although such meetings showed a people uncontrollably seeking escape from and entrance into the great forces that shaped their lives, there was also in their religion a capacity for tenderness. Among their ceremonies was foot washing, where the minister emulated Jesus in humbly serving his disciples. And sermons could reveal a combination of compassion and arresting theology. In the early twentieth century John Campbell heard this story of Abraham and Isaac from a mountain preacher: "Abraham went out in the wilderness on a four days' journey, and he took with him several camels and she-asses and built hisself an altar unto the Lord. And he packed wood hisself for the altar. And Isaac said to Abraham, 'Pap, whar's the ram?' And Abraham said unto Isaac, 'You needn't be worritted about the ram. The Lord will pervide a sacrifice.'

"Then Abraham took his son and stripped him, and he drew his knife"—here the old man paused and his voice grew unconsciously tender—"kindly slow like, don't you reckon, cause it ware his boy, and turned away his head. And the Lord stationed his arm. And there was a ram, catched by his horn in the grapevine!

"I've studied a right smart, and I've asked a heap of men learned in books. What do you reckon would have happened if Abraham had killed Isaac? I reckon there would have been no need to kill

26. A.H. Newman, *A History of the Baptist Churches in the United States* (New York: Christian Literature Co., 1894), 382. Campbell, *Southern Highlander,* 183–87; Dykeman, *The French Broad,* 322–24. Kephart, *Our Southern Highlanders,* 269–71.

Christ. The Scripture says we must be saved by blood, and we would have been saved by the blood of Isaac."[27]

Underlying this compassion there remained, of course, the emphasis on the emotional experience—the direct, uncontrolled personal encounter of man with the unfathomable mysteries of nature and nature's God. This nature, however, did not reveal self-evident truths. It demanded awe and attempts to cope with something that scoffed at understanding. Part of the process of coping was a belief in spirits and omens, in witches and signs and portents, in the right times to plant according to moon phases, in the proper ways to make sure that children were healthy or skilled in some important craft. Kill a wood tick on a baby with a book, and the child will learn to "speak all kind o' proper words." Kill it with an ax or other tool, and the child will be a clever workman; with a banjo string, and the child will master the instrument. Cure a baby's sore mouth with the breath of a man who has never seen his own father.[28]

The religion of the mountaineer thus brought him release, community, and a sense of oneness with uncontrollable nature. What it seems not to have done was to affect his code of ethics significantly. That code was dependent on self-preservation intertwined with self-righteousness. This combination, nurtured by isolation, independence, and a personal religious code, often encouraged brutality rather than restraining it. Men who would feel conscience-stricken over something like breaking the Sabbath or swearing could commit murder and feel that their souls somehow remained unblemished. The story is told of a preacher who, riding down a ravine, came upon a mountaineer with a rifle, hiding in the bushes:

"What are doing there, my friend?" the preacher asked.

"Ride on, stranger. . . . I'm a waitin' fer Jim Johnson, and with the help of the Lawd, I'm goin' to blow his damn head off."

On another occasion, the leader of a clan engaged in a bloody feud remarked that "I have triumphed agin my enemies time and time agin. The Lord's on my side, and I gets a better Christian ever' year."

This capacity to judge others and find them wanting seems to have been one that many mountain killers possessed. Some folks de-

27. Campbell, *Southern Highlander*, 178.
28. Miles, *Spirit of the Mountains*, 98-102.

served killing, and a man had the right, and maybe even the obligation, to determine who those folks might be. A murderer awaiting
trial announced, "I tell you, sir, as sure as God made apples, a
meaner man never broke the world's bread. The only reason he
hadn't died long ago was that God didn't want him, and the devil
wouldn't have him."[29]

This code of retribution might be strictly followed among men,
but it had its limits. With few exceptions, it did not apply to women
and children. They were immune from its harshness. Men marked
for reprisals were granted temporary reprieves if encountered with
their families. The same distinction that distinguished men and
women in their work helped protect women from the brutalities of
feuding. Children were also excluded. Their helplessness at an early
age was obvious protection. Girls kept their immunity as they grew
up, but boys became men and hence potential targets.[30]

It is difficult to establish a precise age for entry into this aspect of
manhood. Presumably a precocious lad who picked up a gun at an
early age became fair game. Nevertheless, killing a man in his early
teens, on the boundary between childhood and maturity, had to be
explained.

The war would expand the numbers of possible victims. Men of
sixteen and even thirteen would be targets when the Union or Confederate cause lent respectability to acts of personal vengeance.
Boys, not men, might be victims when the horrors of war invaded
the mountain valleys. Even women might face death or torture
then. Yet if the brutality of the war would lower the age of victims, it
could not completely banish the need to justify the violence. Years
after the Shelton Laurel killings, those who justified the deed took
pains to explain that Jasper Chandler, the sixteen-year-old who was
one of the victims, had deserved his fate because he had killed and
robbed just like adults. They found it convenient to forget that
David Shelton, age thirteen, had also died there. No matter how
self-righteous a killer felt, there were some things impossible to explain or justify.[31]

29. Miles, *Spirit of the Mountains,* 58; Kephart, *Our Southern Highlanders,*
272–73. Campbell, *Southern Highlander,* 176–80.
30. Kephart, *Our Southern Highlanders,* 344–45; Campbell, *Southern Highlander,* 112–13.
31. A.P. Gaston, *Partisan Campaigns of Lawrence M. Allen* (Raleigh, N.C.: Ed-

This personal sense of righteousness spanned the Civil War era and frequently overwhelmed whatever regular due process might have required. During the war a group of soldiers moved into Shelton Laurel and surrounded Nance "Granny" Franklin's home. The widowed mother of four sons, she had to watch as the troops opened fire and killed three of her boys. She tried to stop the killings but only succeeded in just missing death herself when a bullet clipped off a lock of her hair. The soldiers left, but revenge lurked awaiting its chance.[32]

After the war it came. A few miles away from Shelton Laurel, men were trying to rebuild Mars Hill College, and masons and carpenters from the region came to help. One day one of the bricklayers got to telling war stories to some students. He told of being in on the Franklin killings and recalled something sort of amusing: "Usually I can knock a squirrel out of a tree at seventy-five yards, but I took aim at that woman, almost close enough to touch her, and all I did was shoot off a piece of her hair."

---

wards, 1894), 25ff. It is difficult to determine if this sort of violence points to the existence of feuding in the pre-Civil War mountains. Most students of the feud place its origins in the postwar period, a product of wartime brutality. Such declarations are made with more assurance than documentation. Richard Brown, *Strain of Violence* (New York: Oxford Univ. Press, 1975), announces that "the evidence is persuasive" that feuding is a postwar phenomenon. His source for the statement turns out to be the Hatfield-McCoy feud, while a previous discussion is of a Texas feud of the postwar period. Little effort seems to have been made to look diligently for prewar feuding.

  The positive evidence for prewar feuding is obscure. Cratis Williams, Rupert Vance, C.C. Colby, and L.C. Glenn all speak of neighborhood quarrels as helping to generate allegiances to the Union or the Confederacy. The interesting thing about these assertions is that they build on top of each other, all resting on a single source. See Williams, "Southern Mountaineer in Fact and Fiction," 25, citing Vance, *The Human Geography of the South,* (Chapel Hill, Univ. of N.C. Press, 1932) 35, citing Colby, *Economic Geography,* (Boston: Ginn and Co., 1931) 246, citing L.C. Glenn, "Physiographic Influences in the Development of Tennessee," *Resources of Tennessee* (April 1915), 44-66. Glenn's article, which devotes one undocumented paragraph to neighborhood quarreling, is in a journal devoted to the geology of Tennessee. And Vance's citing of Colby is misleading because the pages in Colby that are cited were written by Glenn, who refers to his own article for support. Margaret Morley asserts, on the other hand, that "there never existed in the North Carolina mountains the extreme and bloody feuds that distinguished the annals of Virginia and Kentucky." *The Carolina Mountains* (Boston: Houghton Mifflin, 1913), 144, 207-208.

  32. Wellman, *Kingdom of Madison,* 88-89, 94-95; story repeated during interview April 4, 1977, by Mrs. Shelton, who insists that Nance Franklin was not the Confederate sympathizer that Wellman says she was.

One of the students took this story with him when he went back home that weekend to Shelton Laurel. He told it to James Norton, who was Nance Franklin's brother, and Norton offered the student a five-dollar gold piece if he would point out the bricklayer. The student identified the unsuspecting veteran, who retold his story. When he finished, Norton announced, "That was my sister you shot the hair off of, and one of her boys you murdered was named James after me." He pulled a revolver from under his coat, shot the bricklayer in the stomach, and ran away. He was soon arrested, and trial was held in the neighboring county.

Nance Franklin rode through the mountains to testify on behalf of her brother. Her descendants remember the testimony vividly, and the jury and spectators at the time were moved, too. Especially memorable was her answer when the judge asked, "Madam, you tell us that you sent your young sons out to fight and kill and be killed. Did you bring them up for that sort of thing?"

"I brought them up as Christians," she answered. "I told them, always be good boys, tell the truth, and be honest. But I told them something else. If you've got to die, die like a damned dog with your teeth in a throat." The jury decided that the victim deserved killing. James Norton went free.[33]

The Sheltons, too, passed personal verdicts of life and death. Perhaps the cause was self-righteousness, perhaps self-preservation, perhaps simple viciousness, but the result was the same. In late May 1854, the *Asheville Spectator* ran this story: "A citizen of Madison County tells us that Tilman, Landers, James Shelton, and another Shelton went to the house of Drury Norton in Laurel one night last week and run him out of his home. After they got him out of the house, they commenced an assault upon him with rocks and so beat and wounded him that he died two or three days afterwards. The perpetrators of this horrid deed have all fled the county, a number of the citizens. . . have gone in pursuit of them and it is hoped they will be arrested — Mr. Norton has left a large family." History has hidden the reason for this murder. Maybe Mr. Norton, despite the size of his family, deserved killing. Apparently the two Sheltons and their associates felt that he did, and acting on that feeling, dispensed justice.[34]

33. Ibid.
34. As quoted in Salisbury *Carolina Watchman,* June 1, 1854.

The personal quality of justice and revenge in the region was starkly revealed during the Civil War, with tragic consequences for the Sheltons themselves. When the Confederate Army began its operations against Unionists in the Shelton Laurel region, it looked for a guide who would point out the pathways and identify the enemy. The man the Confederates found was named Hackley Norton. After the war the pattern of personal revenge continued. A man named David Shelton would kill Norton.[35]

The tendency to see justice in personal terms involved people from throughout the region. Union private Frank Wilkeson was assigned to a refugee camp at Stevenson, Alabama, to help women and children starved or driven out of southern Appalachia. From the refugees he heard stories of crops destroyed, homes burned, husbands murdered. The women did not confine the telling to sympathetic outsiders. "I heard them repeat over and over to their children the names of men which they were never to forget, and whom they were to kill when they had sufficient strength to hold a rifle," Wilkeson recalled. "These women, who had been driven from their homes by the most savage warfare our country has been cursed with, knew what war was, and they impressed me as living wholly to revenge their wrongs."[36]

More than simple self-righteousness was involved in the personal views of justice held by mountaineers. The power of kinship, the isolation of the place, and a highly developed individual sense of right and wrong all contributed to private justice and did so in a complex way. At issue was not a simple balancing of personal vengeance against the rule of law represented by the judicial system. The local courts—located sixteen twisting, rugged miles away in Marshall, the county seat—did not necessarily dispense an impersonal justice.

The judicial and political system of each county was in the hands of the justices of the peace. Once they had been nominated by their local assemblymen and endorsed by the state legislature, these officials might serve for life. They ran the local magistrates courts,

35. W.H. Bailey to Governor Vance, Feb. 18, 1863, Vance Papers, North Carolina State Archives, Raleigh, N.C.; interview with Mrs. Paul Wallin Shelton, Shelton Laurel, N.C., April 4, 1977.
36. Frank Wilkeson, *Recollections of a Private Soldier* (New York: Putnam, 1887), 232–35.

which handled all civil actions under one hundred dollars. They also staffed the county courts, which handled large civil actions and crimes for which death or dismemberment was not the penalty. They called whomever they chose as a jury. The county court also handled administrative duties and appointed officers who levied taxes, licensed the selling of liquor, kept the roads in repair, and performed all other official duties. The superior court handled major felonies and was presided over by a legislatively appointed judge who held court twice a year. This court picked its jury from the citizens in town on court day. The only locally elected officers were constables and sheriffs. It was not a system to inspire the allegiance of rural mountaineers.[37]

Juries in county seats could and did ignore the law and evidence to acquit or convict people they liked or disliked, people whose values or whose kin they did or did not respect. There was no real sense of community between Marshall and Shelton Laurel, between the more metropolitan towns and the traditional communities.[38] Therefore, justice, or the appearance of justice, might not be available from a court of law. As one mountaineer put it, "It doesn't make any difference what the evidence is, the case goes the way they want it to go. Then there is nothing for me to do but to accept and let them throw off on me as a coward, if I stay in the country; to leave the country and give up all I own, and still be looked at as a coward; or to get my kinfolk and friends together and clean up on the other crowd. What would you do?"[39]

Although Shelton Laurel seemed not to have had much experience with clan warfare, it was ruled by the same principle: private justice could be more just than the verdicts of a court. This principle existed when community standards could be applied to members of

37. Ralph Wooster, *Politicians, Planters, and Plain Folk: Courthouse and State-house in the Upper South, 1850-1860* (Knoxville: Univ. of Tennessee Press, 1975), 106-07, 118-27. Johnson, *Ante-Bellum North Carolina,* 620-25. Behavior in the courtroom did not inspire the respect of some lawyers either. In 1854 A.S. Merrimon recorded in his journal, "I have seldom seen such scenes as I have seen today — only two or three cases have been disposed of and they have been *handled* in the rudest manner. The more I see of the County Courts, the more I wish to see them abolished. Drunkenness has reigned today. A portion of the Court has been drunk all day." A.R. Newsome, "The A.S. Merrimon Journal, 1853-1854," *North Carolina Historical Review* 8 (July 1931), 329.
38. Campbell, *Southern Highlander,* 111-12.
39. Ibid.

a community, when the rules of a way of life in a particular place were factors in decisions to punish or not. When people shared values and shared lives, justice outside the courts might claim to be at least as just as that which courts dispensed. The order of custom might be preferable to the rule of law.[40]

Such a possibility diminished when strangers encountered each other. Then personal decisions about who did or did not deserve punishment could not arise from shared values. A man might not be judged by a jury of his peers — by men who shared values about the ends and means of justice. In fact, he might be judged by people who thought that his values and his style of living did not deserve respect.

As isolated communities touched the outside world, the need for a system of due process arose — a way to ensure that evidence would not be submerged in personal bias, that in fact there would be evidence before conviction and conviction before punishment — a way, in short, to make sure that those who deserved killing were the ones who got killed; that those officials who did the killing did so according to a standard of justness that ensured the respect of one person for another regardless of differences.

However, the legal institutions that came to replace traditional practice in dispensing justice were not themselves free of the influence of social custom. Frequently such customs, which viewed outsiders or people who were different as inferior, wrapped themselves in the clothing of the legal system and executed prejudice in the name of due process. And the power of the state was there to enforce prejudice as "the rule of law." Law might be the rule of whoever got control of the courts. Naturally, those who controlled the legal system decided that private vengeance outside the courtroom was inferior to private justice inside. Sometimes this was true; sometimes it was not.

Up in the mountains, far away from the courthouse, people had strong suspicions about the official legal and political system. Such suspicion was the composite of so many differences between town and countryside that it cannot be blamed only on different ideas about how to dispense justice. The important difference was in life

40. My argument here rests on Stanley Diamond, "The Rule of Law Versus the Order of Custom," in *The Rule of Law,* ed. Robert Paul Wolff (New York: Simon and Schuster, 1971), 115-44, and authorities cited there.

style, a distinction about what life was about. If the difference between mountain people was one of degree, the degree was large, and as the mountain town was absorbed into the modern world and the isolation of highlanders increased, the difference grew.

Evolving first as trading centers, mountain towns began to attract people whose life styles, hopes, fears, ambitions, and relationships to the surrounding vastness differed from those of the countryside. In the towns there was less correspondence between men and nature; people looked outside the mountains for needs and plans. The rhythms of their lives reflected the tempo of men grasping for control of their destinies. Of course, townsfolk continued to be mountain people. Not everything about the mountains bored them or stirred their discontent. Mountain townspeople seem to have stayed in the mountains rather than leaving them entirely. So the spirit of the mountains remained in both rural and "urban" people. Nevertheless, the towns were magnets for those who were discontented with traditional values, and people drawn to them met people from other places, with different goals, who offered opportunity, a chance to better themselves, a chance to be something different from the people of Shelton Laurel.

By contrast, the Sheltons in 1860 were entwined with the mountains. Although three Shelton families lived outside the valley, the other twenty families lived within it and had lived there for three generations, since the time in the 1790s when the place had been taken from the Indians. The Sheltons multiplied and, as they did, gradually spread up the valleys and into the hollows. They did not leave this place they had found, even though the land had to be divided into smaller and smaller pieces as the number of children grew. There was much more land available to people who left, but still they stayed.

They stayed despite a widespread poverty among the families. Only four Shelton families owned more than $1,000 in property in 1860. Over half the households owned less than $100. In the third-poorest county in the state, where the per capita wealth for whites was $239, the Sheltons existed on a third of that. And still they stayed.

David's wife, Elizabeth, had been born in South Carolina. James's Sallie was from Kentucky. Seventy-year-old Katherine had been born in Tennessee and so had William Shelton. All the other

133 Sheltons had been born in North Carolina, probably in the Shelton Laurel.

Family ties were strong. Not only did the Sheltons live predominantly in the same valley—making them neighbors as well as kin—but daughters who lost their husbands would return to their parents, and their children would come too. If they were not always in the same household, they were living nearby. Or a widow, if she lived alone, would be helped by a mother-in-law who lived in.

Households usually were large. Sifus led the list with his family of twelve, and the average household contained six or seven people. One of the cabins, however, held only Peter, his wife, Elizabeth, and Coan, age two. Girls began to have children when they were in their late teens, on the average, although some began as early as fifteen. But it was fitting that the Sheltons entered adulthood early because they would leave it soon. Life was short. Only four of the 137 Sheltons listed in the 1860 census were over forty![41]

These were the people of Shelton Laurel, bound in a place they loved, where they abided and planned to remain, living in rhythm with the seasons and the cycle of life, and guided by a personal sense of right and wrong that seemed validated daily because it was shared by everyone they knew and loved and was part of a fabric of life that wove people and place together. They were so isolated from the forces of the modern world that they even spoke a language that visitor Cecil Sharp called "English, not American . . . the language of a past day." While most were illiterate, they sustained an oral tradition participated in by everyone who could sing or tell tales.[42]

Of course, even in the 1850s and 1860s the mountaineers of the Shelton Laurel region were not totally isolated in a physical sense. Although their farms supplied most of their needs, they did have to leave the valley for salt, and from time to time they might go to the nearest village store to barter for manufactured goods. Occasionally peddlers would pass by, selling pins, needles, scissors, and thread, along with ribbons or perfume. Near the foot of the valley, where Shelton Laurel Creek joined Little Laurel Creek, ran a detour off the so-called French Broad Turnpike. In the fall large herds of pigs and cattle were driven by there on their way from Tennessee

41. Manuscript Census, Madison County, N.C., 1860.
42. Campbell and Sharp, *English Folk Songs,* iv–vii.

into the piedmont of North and South Carolina. The main turnpike itself was five miles away from the juncture of the creeks, beyond a ridge and beside the French Broad itself. Here even larger droves of livestock were pushed along to the South, and a stage line competed for the right-of-way, usually without success. Also along this road was the well-known summer resort of Warm Springs, visited by wealthy lowland slave owners. It was about seven miles away from Shelton Laurel. People from the high valleys could reach out to the world too. Men seeking work might find it outside the valley picking fruits and nuts in the orchards of eastern Tennessee. They might take corn to be ground at nearby mills. And whole families might go to town on court days or on rare shopping visits.[43]

Although the mountaineers in Shelton Laurel and other places in the southern Appalachians might reach the outside world when necessary, it was not something they had to do very often or could do with ease. Even the French Broad Turnpike was often impassable, especially when the river rose, and was always filled with rocks and plagued by unsafe bridges. Searching for Unionists in December 1861 in the Laurel region, a Confederate colonel reported, "That country consists of a tumultuous mass of steep hills wooded at the top, with execrable roads winding through ravines and often occupying the bed of a water course." Things were the same ten years later when a traveler noted that "the Laurel Creek Valley was isolated among the mountains and could be reached only by bridle paths."[44]

In such a place it is hardly surprising that the people had no contacts with banks, railroads, or any large commercial places at all. The fact that Madison County listed no manufacturing establishments in the 1860 census further suggests the rural and self-sufficient nature of the place. In 1860 only three bank companies operated in the North Carolina mountains, and they were in Asheville; one was local and the other two were branches of banks in Raleigh and Wil-

43. Gene Wilhelm, Jr., "Appalachian Isolation: Fact or Fiction," in *An Appalachian Symposium: Essays Written in Honor of Cratis D. Williams* (Boone, N.C.: Appalachian State Univ. Press, 1977), 77–91; Forrest McDonald and Grady Mc-Whiney, "The Antebellum Southern Herdsman: A Reinterpretation," *Journal of Southern History* 41 (May 1975), 147–66; Wellman, *Kingdom of Madison,* 38–51. Olmsted, *Journey in the Back Country,* 251; Eller, "Land and Family," 83–95.

44. *OR,* ser. 2, vol. 1, 853; *New York Tribune,* Aug. 10, 1871; William D. Cotton, "Appalachian North Carolina," 44–45.

mington. Asheville, which would not get a railroad line until 1881, was a two-day ride from Shelton Laurel.[45]

The isolation of the mountaineers was not just geographic, it was psychological as well. The people of the high valleys and hollows were stigmatized by outsiders as ignorant, poor, and almost uncivilized. As early as 1853, A.S. Merrimon, who had been born and lived in the more settled regions of the mountains, reported his experiences while visiting circuit court sessions at Jewell Hill, about ten miles from Shelton Laurel. "I do not know any rival for this place in regard to drunkenness, ignorance, superstition and the most brutal debauchery," he wrote one day in October. And the next day: "What degradation!" Appalled by the drunkenness, prostitution, and vulgarity around him, he did not change his mind three months later: "As is usual for this place, drunkenness is carried on to an incredible extent . . . a wretched state of morals."[46]

The Civil War experience fed this image. Although the brutality of mountain warfare had yet to reach major proportions, an observer in the winter of 1861 described a group of women whose husbands were being sought as "in some cases greatly alarmed, throwing themselves on the ground and wailing like savages. Indeed," he added, "the population is savage." The commander of the Department of East Tennessee, Kirby Smith, agreed. In April 1862 he pictured the Unionists of this region as "an ignorant, primitive people." Five years after Appomattox a merchant in Marshall asserted that the people surrounding the town were "too ignorant to govern themselves." And a visitor described "cabins . . . invariably without windows, and from each there swarmed a numerous brood of half clad, unkempt, tow headed children. . . . It is hard to say how their inhabitants subsist. They seem to have nearly solved the problem of how to live upon nothing; for beside their wretched little break-neck cornfields, they have no visible means of subsistence."[47]

By the Civil War era the people of Shelton Laurel, like mountaineers in other parts of the South, had become isolated, despite the

45. Cotton, "Appalachian North Carolina," 36–38, 55–62; Joseph Carlyle Sitterson, *The Secession Movement in North Carolina* (Chapel Hill: Univ. of North Carolina Press, 1939), 18–21; United States Census of Manufacturers, 1860, pp. 436–37. In the entire mountain region of North Carolina there were only 192 manufacturing places, averaging two employees each.

46. Newsome, "The A.S. Merrimon Journal, 1853–1854," 310–11, 325–26.

47. *OR*, ser. 2, vol. 1, 853; ser. 1, vol. 10, 386; *New York Tribune*, Aug. 10, 1871.

fact that a few avenues were open to them to take part in a larger world. They chose to remain where they were, to turn their backs on the outside world rather than participate in it. The geography of their place made this choice an easy one, and so did the satisfaction they apparently gained in so choosing.

They paid a price for this isolation. The relative poverty and ignorance that they thereby accepted made it easy for outsiders to see them as inferior, primitive, degraded. Choosing not to take part in the outside world was an implicit criticism of that world, and they earned the resentment of those they seemed to criticize. They also paid a price for retaining values that were losing dominance in the world around them. The growing influence of the slave economy attracted to it wealthy and ambitious men who retained and nurtured ties to the outside world. Large farmers could foresee selling food and tobacco to the piedmont and plantation markets. Villages might become commercial centers, expanding the wealth and influence of their leaders.

As the power of slavery grew, men in the statehouse and the courthouse who had political ambitions were drawn to the support of what became the Confederate South. Of course, older allegiances retained their claims as well. Few mountaineers rushed headlong into the secession cause, but the strength of new allegiances would make their Unionism more conditional than their devotion to the Confederacy. Lacking involvement in such newer forces, most highland rural mountaineers would not develop new allegiances. But men in the towns and villages and wealthier farmers, along with some of the newer class of tenant farmers dependent on the wealthy owners, were more easily made into supporters of the new Confederate nation. It was in Marshall, the center for the wealthier and more ambitious people of Madison County, that these forces were most strongly felt, and it was in Marshall that James A. Keith and Lawrence M. Allen were making their mark.[48]

48. Williams, "Southern Mountaineer in Fact and Fiction," 22–25; Wilhelm, "Appalachian Isolation," 88–90; Wooster, *Politicians, Planters and Plain Folk,* passim.

THE OFFICERS
AND
THE GENERAL

It should not be that men of enlarged intelligence should make a civil war more desperate than it is sure to be made by . . . a class of soldiers who all their lives have been used to the largest amount of liberty to do their will, good or bad. You know full well that on your side guerrillas or partisan rangers commit acts which you would not sanction, and that small detachments of our men commit acts of individual revenge, leaving no trace whereby we can fix responsibility. Instead of yielding to this tendency we ought gradually to improve discipline so that each general in command can trace all acts and then assume responsibility. If we allow the passions of our men to get full command then indeed will this war become a reproach to the names of liberty and civilization.

WILLIAM T. SHERMAN TO
T.C. HINDEMAN
October 17, 1862

Something in James Keith would not rest. He had to be improving himself, working his way up, becoming somebody. For him the land was not enough. The seasons and the harmony with the place did not satisfy him. Maybe his father, a Baptist preacher, had something to do with that. Sometimes preachers taught more than resignation. Sometimes the idea crept in that a man had a calling and should see about that calling, that God had given each person gifts and a man did not waste God's gift by letting it lie fallow. Keith's father was an example to him, too—doing his duty for his flock, seeking them out, moving from place to place to spread the word of the Lord, going about His work striving, always striving, to be better in His eyes. And

31

maybe there was something in having books around and being able to read them and having to study the Word, not just hear it spoken.

Keith also might have been driven by the fact that his father had made something of himself and become comparatively well-off by the standards of the mountain people he ministered to. The other Keiths generally did pretty well too. One kinsman, Alfred, had made about $2,000 while James was growing up. Another, John, was one of the rare slave owners in the county, as far back as 1840. Also possibly contributing to Keith's ambition was the fact that the Lord seemed not to be displeased by wealth among mountain ministers. Keith's father had substantial holdings, and a little ways down the road lived another Baptist minister named Metcalf who was one of the richest men in the county.

Whatever the sources of his ambition, in the decade before the Civil War James Keith improved himself. Starting in 1850 as a twenty-three-year old laborer, in ten years he had become a doctor and a farmer. By the time he was thirty-two, he was among the twenty wealthiest people in Madison County. Living in Marshall, he was surrounded by other people with wealth.

He had two children, Laura, three, and baby Douglas, not quite a year old when the war broke out. Keith also took into his home young Mitchell Keith whose father had died, leaving about $2,000 in property. He was trying to ensure that Mitchell would make something of himself by sending the young man to school. Also living in and further symbolizing Keith's status was a Negro hired man named Isiah Foster.[1]

Keith clearly was a young man with a promising future and a family to help him share that success. Educated, wealthy, he could look forward to a life of influence and responsibility, to being in control of a promising destiny. Perhaps there would be some glory to adorn it, for when the Civil War began, it was to the James Keiths of the South that the Confederates looked to organize regiments and lead them to victories.

Lawrence M. Allen was a man with a future too. He had wanted to better himself and by 1860 was doing so. He had been fortunate enough to start from a well-to-do foundation. His father, Riley, was

1. Manuscript Census, Buncombe, Yancy Counties, N.C., 1850; Madison County, N.C., 1860.

a substantial farmer when Lawrence was born in 1833. His mother being from Spartanburg, South Carolina, suggests that Riley was the sort of man who traveled beyond the mountains around him. Heritage also gave Allen something to live up to. Family tradition claimed that his ancestors had played important roles in the American Revolution.[2]

These elements conspired to push young Allen to achievements that began as soon as he entered school. He was an outstanding student, always at the head of his class, and in a mountain school that fact set him off from other students, especially the poorer, more rural ones.

To the rural people, school was a place to go to when other matters did not press. Sometimes their children went, and sometimes they did not. They learned what the teacher told them as well as they could, but their lives would go on pretty much as before even if they did not learn. They were courteous and well behaved in the classroom, but everyone, teachers as well as classmates, understood that things outside the classroom were what really mattered. There were things that the mountains taught and that the seasons, the animals, and the need to help out at home taught them to be of abiding importance. The only book that truly mattered was the Bible, and God still spoke to them even if they could not read it. He was there in the stars and in the wilderness, in loneliness and the need for consolation when folks died, and in the awesome beauty of the place. He was there and the Book might help explain some things, but they knew what He wanted and what life required. So the need to read, figure, and write did not press hard. Indeed, too much reading and book learning might make children forget who and what they were and where they came from.[3]

Lawrence Allen excelled in school by his energy, his obedience,

2. Gaston, *Partisan Campaigns of Allen,* 5–6.
3. Campbell, *Southern Highlander,* 268, 285; Olmsted, *Journey in the Back Country,* 238. The 1860 census listed 31 of the 55 Sheltons over age sixteen as illiterate: 19 women and 12 men. Also listed were 22 of 39 children between ages seven and sixteen as having attended school in the past year. The listing of illiterates seems incomplete. Attendance at school could mean anything from a perfect attendance record to having made one visit. On the average, wealthier Sheltons were more likely to send their children to school. While the poorest family to send children to school held $10 in property, the average for such households was about $1,260. The weathiest family not to send a child to school held $2,000, but the average for nonsending families with eligible children was about $345.

and his ambition. He meant to live up to what school required of him and to succeed, to make the most of chances that life sent his way and become wealthy and important, to make himself someone who mattered.

One of the ways to do that was to marry well, and in 1853 Allen wedded Mary Peek. The bride's father had been in the Mexican War and was a sort of hero in the area. There were other credentials too. Wealth and education were talked of in her family. She was what the folks in the region called "of excellent standing," and that bauble exalted her husband.

He helped himself too. During the late 1850s he began acquiring property in and around Marshall, and by 1860 he was worth almost $5,000, which made him a man of considerable means, given the poverty of the county. Further signs of his status were the two servants who lived in his home and the fact that his five-year-old daughter and even his three-year-old son were sent to school.[4]

Allen also used politics to advance himself. He ran for clerk of the superior court of Madison County and won. He kept on winning because he worked hard at his job. He took an active part in Democratic party politics in the county and was consistently a delegate to the state party convention. Like Keith, Allen was a man to be reckoned with.[5]

When war broke out, Allen again saw opportunity. Perhaps someone so well treated by his region swelled with patriotism after Sumter. Surely a man with so much invested in the state government and politics had something to defend. And perhaps the image of himself as an officer, a leader, and a man of achievement stirred him to action. He enlisted under his wife's kinsman, John Peek, almost as soon as the echoes of Sumter's cannons reached Marshall. He served a few months under Peek's command, but by July of 1861 he was back in Marshall organizing his own company of 125 men who unanimously chose him their captain. Allen, like Keith, was ready for war.[6]

Other men had been prepared in different ways. The war would need not only colonels and privates to do the killing, but generals to give the necessary orders, to command as well as excuse the killing. In the Shelton Laurel killings the general was Henry Heth.

4. Manuscript Census, Madison County, N.C., 1860.
5. Gaston, *Partisan Campaigns of Allen,* 6.
6. Ibid.

Henry Heth was a Virginia gentleman's son who became a general. The Old Dominion spawned many such men, born and raised in a social system that made them accustomed to giving orders, as well as taking responsibility for those they gave orders to. The environment fostered the attitude of command, if not the actual talent for it. They knew how to act like leaders, whether or not they actually could lead or not. Some led inspirationally, gaining love as well as obedience. Some simply found themselves in positions of leadership.[7]

The Heth family wealth came from agriculture and mining, as well as from manufacturing. His father owned a large plantation, coal mines, and a textile and paper company. It was a blending of old station with new wealth. The Heths, if not first family, were at least second family of Virginia. Henry's position made him a cousin of George Pickett, a family friend of Henry Wise, and of the prominent state businessmen, Gouverneur Kimble and William G. McNeill. It was a good life. There was fox hunting, game shooting, vacations at White Sulphur Springs, and a special devotion by Henry's father to horse breeding and racing. There were social gatherings with the leading families of Virginia, and for Henry there was training at prep schools to prepare him for college and the life of a gentleman.[8]

Then at seventeen, at a point in life when he was to take the first serious steps toward his career, Heth suffered a personal loss that shook him profoundly. The death of his father was "the most severe calamity I had ever felt." His father had been not only a parent but also a companion in recreation whose talent easily awed his son. He was an expert marksman and a superb horseman. Throughout his life Henry Heth would cultivate the same talents in himself. Indeed, he would blend the two. While serving on the frontier, he taught himself to hunt buffalo on horseback with revolvers. On one occasion he would kill seven buffalo with seven shots while riding full speed beside a running herd.[9]

Aside from the personal loss of a father and an idol, there were other consequences as well. His father's death seriously weakened

7. James L. Morrison, Jr., ed., *Memoirs of Henry Heth* (Westport, Conn.: Greenwood, 1974), 10–12.
8. Ibid.
9. Ibid., 125–26.

the economic foundations for the life style that had shaped Henry's personality. He somehow had to find a career that would support him financially as well as provide him the social position to which he had been born. Something would have to sustain Heth both emotionally and economically. The military was the obvious answer. It would be his home.

Within a year of his father's death, Heth received an appointment to West Point. He also was offered admission to Annapolis, but his mother rejected the navy because she believed that naval officers met more moral temptations than did soldiers. She might have been right, but Henry would soon demonstrate that the difference was one of degree.[10]

Despite his prep school training, Heth's academic progress at the Point was marginal at best. His grades were barely good enough to keep him in school, and he would graduate next to last in his class, in that group called derisively "The Immortals." Experiencing a decline in economic status, the pain of losing his father, and the shock of academic incompetence, Heth found his status in the class of 1847 by becoming its outstanding prankster and general incorrigible. Reprimanded for everything from "laughing in the ranks" and "making improper use of the coal pile" to "vulgar and offensive language" and "neglect of his duty as a sentinel," Heth would finish his years at the academy with a grand total of 683 demerits—an accumulation that placed him next to last in conduct in his class.

Much of his misconduct took the form of hazing underclassmen— usually those poorer and less well stationed than he was. Heth had been protected from intensive hazing as an underclassman by his cousin George Pickett, an upperclassman during Heth's first years, but his own immunity did not make him merciful to others. Joining forces with Ambrose Burnside, Heth delighted in degrading and embarrassing new men. One day the two of them, posing as barbers, managed to give an underclassman exactly one-half of a shave and a haircut, finishing just at the moment inspection was called. On another occasion Heth helped organize a mock bigamy trial of a new cadet from the mountains of North Carolina. "The ugliest, most misshapen plebe I ever saw," Heth later recalled. The sentence for the young man's sin was death. As penance for his crime the

10. Ibid., 13–14.

"court" ordered him to stand in the yard with his head in a cannon until called for execution. An officer discovered the cadet in the morning and gave him a severe reprimand.[11]

Heth's other pranks included the theft or at least extended borrowing of horses, food, and wine, general carousing at local taverns, and post-curfew visits with neighborhood women. On one of these occasions he was saved from dismissal only by the fact that the lady in question came from a highly respectable family and officials feared public embarrassment for the family if Heth were disciplined.[12]

In later years the general showed little remorse for his undistinguished West Point career. He reported his pranks gleefully and admitted that what he chiefly enjoyed about the beginnings of his army career were the hell-raising and the impression that a handsome Virginia gentleman in uniform made on young women.[13]

Heth's rank in his graduating class ensured his assignment as a lieutenant in the infantry; artillery and especially cavalry duties went to high achievers. He was sent to Mexico in February of 1848 but missed combat in the Mexican War. Shortly after he arrived, the peace treaty was on its way to Washington. A few guerrillas still roamed the countryside, but Heth never encountered them. However, there were enough veterans of the fighting around to tell unblooded soldiers what fighting meant. The stories about guerrilla fighting were especially gruesome, and not just on the Mexican side.[14]

In the winter of 1846, for example, Generals William Worth and Zachary Taylor entered Saltillo, a town near Buena Vista, and began an occupation. It was tedious duty by volunteer citizen soldiers among an alien and comparatively poor population. Military discipline sagged in such conditions. Having enlisted to fight for glory, the soldiers were not pleased with having to police the grounds. They sought out trouble and found it. Local citizens were harassed, robbed, and sometimes murdered. One volunteer wrote that "plundering is getting pretty common and often with bad results. Recently an old gray bearded sheep herder was shot because he objected to the shooting of his sheep." By January of 1847 the head of the Arkansas regiment was getting strong letters from General John

11. Ibid., 29–30.
12. Ibid.
13. Ibid., 18.
14. Ibid.

Ellis Wool, in charge of the volunteers, denouncing him for the depredations of his troops. Most of the regular soldiers considered the volunteer officers to be incapable of controlling their men among this foreign population.[15]

Mexican guerrillas demonstrated that brutality knew no nationality. Brigadier General José Urrea showed the character of irregular warfare in February 1847 when his cavalry joined up with guerrillas to attack a pack train bringing supplies to the American army. The few Americans guarding the train were easily overwhelmed, and the Mexican force murdered forty or fifty of the teamsters, probably to discourage enlistments of trained drivers. A month later the Texas Rangers replied in kind. On March 28 they murdered twenty-four Mexicans at Rancho Guadaloupe. Private soldiers took their revenge on other suspected guerrillas some time later. When local authorities released the accused guerrillas from jail because of lack of evidence against them, the soldiers ambushed the freed men and killed them.

Atrocity followed atrocity in the guerrilla warfare that raged throughout 1847. Mexicans killed civilians and soldiers alike in attacks on provision trains. Americans repaid the killing of a well-liked major near Huamantla by raping, pillaging, and murdering civilians when their officers allowed them to sack the town. Guerrillas replied by torturing unfortunate Americans who fell into their hands. A man might find himself "lassoed, stripped naked, and dragged through stumps of cactus until his body was full of needle-like thorns; then his privates cut off and crammed into his mouth . . . left to die in the [desert] or to be eaten alive by coyotes."[16]

These were the experiences and stories that instructed officers who were soon to join regiments dealing with Indians and later to cope with guerrillas in the Civil War. Although the regular soldiers seem to have behaved well, the short-term enlistees and irregulars compiled a record of brutality against so-called greasers that was hard to forget.

Heth's encounter with "guerrillas" was a comic adventure. Riding

15. K. Jack Bauer, *The Mexican War, 1846–1848* (New York: Macmillan, 1974), 204.

16. Ibid., 218–23, 333; *House Executive Documents,* 30th Cong., 1st sess., 60, p. 1178; 56, pp. 328–33; John Edward Weems, *To Conquer a Peace* (Garden City, N.Y.: Doubleday, 1974), 281.

out on patrol one day, the eager lieutenant spotted what looked like a band of fifty guerrillas moving toward some deadly deed. Heth charged the band and discovered that it consisted of two old Mexicans leading a train of fifty donkeys taking wood to a nearby town. Adding to his embarrassment, his horse panicked when one of the donkeys unexpectedly squealed and he was forced to flee. He recalled reporting to the commander this "insult to our flag" and asking for the chance to "return and annihilate those two greasers." The colonel replied, "Take your place in the column, sir, you have done all I wished you to do." "Too tender hearted," Heth thought to himself, "and too old to have a sweetheart at home."[17]

Mexico had not given Heth a first-hand encounter with war. Rather, his experience taught him more subtle things. The brutality of guerrilla warfare was one. The other thing he learned was that the Mexicans were a "nation of blanketed thieves" who delighted in the cruelty of bullfighting and "killed and robbed any helpless soldier found alone." Heth's racial views were hardly unique to him. They fit the pattern of American views of Mexicans. However, Heth now had the personal experience that would give authority to his opinions not only before others but also to himself. Somehow it was easy to pool impressions so that guerrillas were "greasers," were thieves and killers, and one had thus captured the essence of the Mexican race.[18]

In 1851 the army sent Heth to Fort Atkinson, near the present Dodge City, Kansas. His assignment was to preserve peace with the Indians and to protect travelers going west. Frontier duty brought white soldiers face to face with another "uncivilized" race. Outside northern Europe and Canada it would have been difficult to find a race not defined by nineteenth-century Americans as inferior in civilization to themselves, and the Plains Indians were ranked at the lower end of the spectrum.[19]

Different ways of life ensured misunderstanding and blocked the possibility of changing this attitude. Especially troublesome were the differing concepts of personal and group responsibility. Whites saw the Plains Indians as nomadic, which contrasted with their own

17. Morrison, *Memoirs of Heth,* 54–55.
18. Ibid.
19. Ibid.

desires to own and occupy land. Although whites prided themselves on their individualism, they also organized permanent political communities and respected laws originating in those places as part of a social fabric for which all citizens were responsible. Indian culture, of course, had its rules and laws too, but whites could not perceive the nature of that order and concluded that Indians were politically irresponsible and subject to the commands of unreliable nomadic chiefs.[20]

Few army or civilian leaders were sensitive to the ways in which army actions were responsible for the disruptions experienced on the frontier. Only in subtle ways was their sensitivity to what they were doing to the Indians reflected. Having stolen Indian land, lied in treaties, and encouraged extermination of tribes, whites quickly branded Indians as thieves, liars, and savages. But there was little time or inclination to investigate such ironies. The army was interested in its ability to control the Indians, in what sort of power Indians had, in how they would fight if it came to that. The structure of Indian society and the vast difference in firepower guaranteed that any fighting would be guerrilla warfare.

In Plains Indian warfare bands of from five to thirty braves would strike without warning, hold no position, seek no territorial objective. The bands attacked to get booty, to avenge a wrong, to gain personal glory, or retaliate for an attack. Avoiding pitched battles against the better equipped white soldiers, they would hit and run and then hide. Their nomadic life blended with their guerrilla tactics and made retaliation by organized soldiers practically impossible. "In a campaign against Indians," one veteran wrote, "the front is all around, and the rear is nowhere." Kirby Smith recalled the futility of the search for a Comanche chief named Sanaco: "We traveled through the country, broke down our men, killed our horses, and returned as ignorant of the whereabouts of Mr. Sanaco as when we started." As historian Robert Utley puts it, "One fruitless disheartening pursuit after another made up by far the largest share of the soldiers' field service."[21]

The frustrations of the situation were intensified by the ambiguous status of the enemy. By 1850 most tribes had treaties with the

20. Robert Utley, *Frontiersmen in Blue: The United States Army and the Indian, 1848-1865* (New York: Macmillan), 8-9.
21. Ibid., 110.

United States and thus by legal definition were allies, not enemies. The army faced the sporadic hostility of individuals within a nominally friendly tribe, and its role thus became more that of a police force than a military one. Further frustrating was the fact that an allegedly friendly tribe might be privately encouraging the hostilities.[22]

So, besides enduring the boredom, the low pay, the bad food and quarters, the cold, heat, dust, mud, and fatigue, men in the frontier army seldom had the chance to vent their frustrations, to gain the distinction or feel the triumph of man-to-man, fight-to-the-finish combat. Their apparent friends might be merely deceitful enemies, and their undoubted enemies they could not catch. The atmosphere begged for resolution.

Although Heth surely felt this frustration and suffered the inconvenience of frontier duty, he would later recall these years as the most pleasant of his life. He was growing to maturity and finding an arena for his talents and satisfaction of his needs. He was commanding officer at Fort Atkinson. He controlled his own fate to a large extent and made decisions on the spot.

Furthermore, he found in the West a place where he could live out the role his father had played, as generous host to passing travelers and visiting army classmates, as skilled horseman and seldom erring marksman. All these were things he had loved in his father, and now he could take his father's place, rule his "plantation," revel in his skills. Army life was providing much more than just a career.

There were obvious differences between being the lord of a Virginia manor and the commander of a wood fort in frontier Kansas, but Heth did with what he had. He rode down buffalo herds, pistols blazing. He hunted antelope, deer, wolves, and jackrabbits with pistols, rifles, and even bow and arrows. His favorite prey was the buffalo, and he boasted of killing over a thousand of them while stationed in the West.[23]

Although Heth found joys on the western prairies, his job was Indian control and he paid serious attention to it. He approached his task with an awareness of some of the subtleties of Indian relations. He distinguished between the tribes and individual Indians. Despising the Pawnees, he admired the Cheyennes for their courage. He

22. Ibid.
23. Morrison, *Memoirs of Heth,* 83, 103, 108.

informally adopted a Kiowa orphan. Some Indians he knew well enough to call friends — one of them would save his life.

Still and all, he saw Indians as uncivilized. A southern gentleman used to placing women on pedestals, he was especially scornful of the way they treated women. The squaws died at early ages, he believed, worked to death because the braves refused to do any domestic labor. This angered Heth and truly clinched his belief in Indian inferiority. The measure of civilization, he believed, was the way a people treated its women and its old people. Seeing squaws aged by endless work and old people abandoned to die convinced Heth that he was dealing with a low level of humanity.

Furthermore, there was the cruelty, the killing of male captives, the murder of women and children, the scalping of the dead and wounded, the kidnapping of children, and, of course, the constant stealing that these people engaged in. In Heth's eyes the Pawnees matched the Mexicans in this thievery, and he wondered if perhaps the Pawnees were not somehow descended from the Aztecs.[24]

Gradually Heth found his framework for dealing with the Indians. A person could be friendly with individuals, admire some of the tribes, but for the Indian as a race one thing was sure — they understood courage and force. Along with members of the army throughout the plains, Heth gradually devised tactics to respond to the Indian's way of life and especially of war. These tactics evolved from acting as a police force chasing down individual mavericks to acting like an army. They would deal with criminal behavior by members of Indian tribes by punishing the tribe itself.

The tactic was a natural one, growing out the general white tendency to homogenize Indians into a mass, to avoid considering the intricacies of Indian culture, and to avoid having to know too many of the potential enemy as individual people. Military necessity also encouraged the new tactic. How much simpler to strike at an entire tribe than at little bands of quicksilver marauders. The full tribe or bands within the tribe were less mobile, being slowed by women, children, and the old. Furthermore, the new tactic placed responsibility for order on the Indians themselves, in the hands of chiefs who knew their people and presumably were better able to control them. As Utley says, the new tactic "raised the hope that severe

24. Ibid., 52, 92-102.

enough punishment of the group, even though innocent suffered along with the guilty, might produce true group responsibility and end the menace to the frontiers."[25]

In practice the tactic worked like this. If "Indians" were accused of some crime or violation of a treaty, the nearest army post would dispatch soldiers to the camp of the presumed criminal. There the soldiers would demand that the culprit be surrendered. This demand often worked. Armed soldiers in the presence of Indian homes and families tended to be persuasive, but it was a touchy business. The commander had to be sure the Indians were intimidated enough and that his troops were well armed and numerous enough to get in and get out of the camp alive. Occasionally someone miscalculated.

In the summer of 1852 reports came into Fort Atkinson that a white man had been killed by Indians. Heth was ordered to take thirty men and some cannon, ride to the suspected Kiowa village, and bring the offender in. Heth and his troops rode to the village and then into it. The chief was angry at this insult of bringing armed troops into his camp. He began to protest, and Heth looked up to find himself surrounded by about five hundred braves. A massacre impended. Then the young officer's friendship with a Kiowa chief paid off. The man rode into camp, up to Heth, and pointed out that there was one escape route left open and that the soldiers had better take it. Heth agreed and left the village without a shot being fired. Some time later the Kiowas sent the suspect to the soldiers, who ultimately released him.[26]

The dangers of this encounter did little to cool Heth's ardor for this "bristling phalanx" solution to Indian problems. That same winter he heard that the Cheyennes had killed a traveler on the road. He gathered his forces for an attack on the offending village. Only the intervention of trader William Bent stopped the raid. Bent learned that white men, not Indians, were the killers. Heth called off the attack.[27]

The army persisted in this solution to Indian troubles, and in the summer of 1854 it blew up in their faces, or at least in the faces of a

25. Utley, *Frontiersmen in Blue*, 111–12.
26. Morrison, *Memoirs of Heth*, 106–07.
27. Donald J. Berthong, *The Southern Cheyenne* (Norman: Univ. of Oklahoma Press, 1963), 124.

young lieutenant and twenty-nine soldiers. The story began quietly enough. A group of Mormon immigrants to Utah let one of their cows stray and a brave from the Brulé band of the Sioux killed the beast and invited his friends to the party.

The Mormons protested this "outrage," and Lieutenant John L. Gratten, eager to earn his spurs, pushed his commanders for the chance to administer justice. He got his wish. Taking twenty-eight men and an unfortunately drunk interpreter, Gratten rode to the Sioux camp and demanded the thief. The prospective prisoner refused to surrender, and the chief backed him up. Gratten insisted, argued, and then threatened. Meanwhile some four hundred braves were surrounding the soldiers. Finally Gratten's patience ran out. He opened fire with his cannon — and succeeded in blowing the tops off some tepees. The Indians were better shots; within a half hour the entire Gratten party was dead.

The incident angered the Brulés and provoked a national outcry. The Indians took their wrath out on the Salt Lake stage in November 1854, killing three, wounding one, and taking $10,000 in gold. The army began to warn of an impending Indian rampage. Speaking for more reasoned sentiment, Senator Thomas Hart Benton spoke of "a heavy penalty for a nation to pay for a lame Mormon cow and for the folly and juvenile ambition of a West Point fledgling."[28]

The army's response to the Gratten incident was to escalate its efforts — to punish the Brulés. And despite his close call a few years earlier, or maybe because of it, Heth was eager to join the punitive expedition. Appointed captain in early 1855, he jumped at the chance to join General William S. Harney's expedition to teach the "savages" a lesson.

The expedition epitomized the attitudes and tactics toward the red guerrillas during the 1850s, the time of Heth's frontier education. Harney was a hard-swearing, stern, and vigorous soldier who had concluded that the way to deal with Indians was to whip them first and then talk peace. As the expedition left Fort Atkinson, the general remarked, "By God, I'm for battle, no peace."[29]

As the troops marched closer to the Brulés, the attitude endured: savages understood force; whites could give no sign of anything less

28. Lloyd McCann, "The Gratten Massacre," *Nebraska History* 37 (March 1956), 1–26; *Congressional Globe*, 33d Cong., 2d sess., app., p. 339 (Feb. 27, 1855).
29. Utley, *Frontiersmen in Blue,* 115.

than stern manhood. One evening as they moved within two miles of the Brulés, General Harney and Captain Heth were sitting outside the general's tent. A Colonel Cooke approached and asked for the orders for the next day. Heth was astonished to hear Harney say nothing about an attack, only about marching on. As Cooke left, the general turned to the young captain: "I wonder what those damned Indians will say of my not attacking them."

"I know exactly," Heth answered; "they will say they came where you now are, and offered to give the big White Chief, the hornet, as they call you, a fight, but that you tucked your tail between your legs and ran away."

Harney stood up and looked at Heth. "Goddamn them, will they say that, Captain?"

"That is exactly what they will say."

"Colonel Cooke," Harney called.

Cooke returned. "Colonel Cooke, I intend to attack those damned redskins in the morning."

Harney ordered Cooke to take the cavalry and get behind the Brulés during the night. The main force would move on the camp to reach it at dawn. "They will break and run towards you; don't let a damned one escape."[30]

When light came, the men were in place. Harney sent word to the Indians for the chief, Little Thunder, to come out and parley. They talked for about a half hour, the chief claiming he could not give up the suspects, protesting that he was friendly, urgently trying to avoid a fight. At one point he offered his hand to Harney, but the general refused it. One of the officers thought the whole thing a farce. "How far this peaceable and friendly disposition was begotten by the presence of the troops before him, burning to avenge their murdered comrades, cannot be known, but a smaller party doubtless would have met with a different reception."[31]

Finally the parley was over. Little Thunder returned to his people. Harney advanced. The Indians retreated and ran into the trap set for them by Cooke's troops. The soldiers fought and chased the Indians for several miles. At the end of the day all those warriors not lucky enough to get away were killed—about eighty-six in all.

30. Morrison, *Memoirs of Heth,* 127-28.
31. "The Harney Expedition Against the Sioux: The Journal of Captain John B.S. Todd," *Nebraska History* 43 (June 1962), 112.

The army took no male prisoners. Perhaps a dozen women and children were killed and nearly sixty were taken prisoner. When the soldiers rode into what remained of the Indian camp, their suspicions of the low nature of these people were confirmed. They found among the Indian booty, General Harney alleged, "the scalps of two white females, and remnants of the clothing carried off by the Indians in the Gratten massacre; all of which sufficiently characterize the people I have had to deal with."[32]

Heth was there too, running down what he recalled as "about 200 bucks," following riders, revenging the Gratten party, believing that this was what had to be done to teach such people an unforgettable lesson. While Harney was present, the lesson was learned. The Indians called him "The Butcher" and fear reigned where he marched. The long-range result of such tactics, however, would be the precipitation of two decades of frontier warfare with the Sioux and other Plains tribes. Places like Sand Creek, Little Big Horn, and Wounded Knee attested to the consequences of this kind of pedagogy.[33]

By that time, of course, Heth would be far from Indian fighting. Shortly after the Harney expedition, the young captain was assigned to a different place, though not sufficiently changed so that he would be forced to learn much that was new. This time Heth would be able to elaborate his ideas about red versus white relations to white versus white.

In 1858, after further uneventful duty in the Kansas-Nebraska region, his marriage in 1857, and some time spent preparing a manual on rifle firing, Heth reported for assignment to Fort Leavenworth. His new duty was to join General Albert Sidney Johnston in Utah and enforce the laws, protect immigrants, and secure order within the territory. Given the state of relations between the Mormons and the United States government, the task did not appear to be an easy one.

Heth did not go to Utah with an open mind about Mormons. He shared the nation's prejudices, was appropriately shocked at polygamy, and was ready to believe that Brigham Young's people were brutal, lascivious, and deceitful. In short, he was ready to apply to

32. "Report on the Sioux, Expedition of 1855," *Senate Documents,* 34th Cong., 1st sess., no. 1, pt. 2, pp. 50–51; Eugene Bandel, *Frontier Life in the Army* (Glendale: Arthur Clark, 1932), 84–87.
33. Morrison, *Memoirs of Heth,* 127–28.

them all the adjectives he had applied to Mexicans and Indians.[34]

Nothing that he saw in Utah changed his mind. Every prejudice was strengthened, and every experience validated his belief that Mormons should be treated much as Indians were. Arriving at Camp Floyd, situated between Provo and Salt Lake City, Heth encountered the gruesome relics of the Mountain Meadows massacre. After that experience he was unlikely to change his opinions of Mormons.

The massacre had occurred in September 1857. Mormons disguised as Indians had trapped a group of about 130 Oregon emigrants in a mountain pass. Posing as the head of a rescue party, a Mormon leader named John Lee convinced the emigrants to disarm themselves as a sign of good faith to the Indians. After the emigrants complied, Lee's men systematically murdered 120 men, women, and children. They spared only those too young to testify.[35]

Soldiers from Camp Floyd were sent to the scene and returned with the bodies and skeletons of the dead, which apparently were used as part of the orientation program for new arrivals to Mormon country. Heth was already convinced of the moral anarchy of Young's followers, that their leaders employed assassins to murder dissenters, and that Young was "the most evil man God ever made in America." His hatred of Mormons increased.[36]

When Heth left the company of soldiers and met the population itself, his attitudes toward the Saints had no chance to change. The duty that fell to him was a soldier's nightmare. He was assigned to guard prisoners for Federal Judge John Cradelbaugh's court in Provo. Since there was no jail in town adequate to hold prisoners, Heth's detachment set up their prison in a corral across the street from the courthouse. The local population was outraged by the presence of troops within the town. Victims of persecution wherever they had gone, the Mormons saw the troops as simply the vanguard of a massive military onslaught. Furthermore, Cradelbaugh had announced his intention of bringing to justice all those guilty of the Mountain Meadows massacre and everyone responsible for other murders of gentiles that had recently been committed. Mormons did

34. Ibid.
35. Juanita Brooks, *The Mountain Meadows Massacre* (Palo Alto, Calif.: Stanford Univ. Press, 1950).
36. Morrison, *Memoirs of Heth,* 143–45.

not expect much justice in Cradelbaugh's court. When the judge subsequently had the mayor of the town arrested for murder, the town became a powder keg. Men swarmed in from the surrounding countryside to protect their leader and to harass the troops. Heth and his men became the focus of their hatred. Surrounded by outraged citizens who were not quite an opposing army, yet certainly not passive bystanders, the soldiers felt increasing fear and frustration.

From inside and outside the courtroom came more signs of the insecurity of the position. The local juries would not convict or even indict suspects. Heth thought they were getting direct orders from Brigham Young. The townspeople began to harass his men, taunting them, then escalating the violence — throwing rocks at his sentries. Heth warned the mayor, "Should this be repeated, I will regret the consequences that will ensue." The rocks kept flying. Then, his patience gone, Heth lashed out. He issued a proclamation "warning the Mormons if this continued, my guards had received instructions to fire."[37]

Fortunately the troops were not forced to fire. The situation remained heated for a time but gradually cooled down when Cradelbaugh adjourned his court, frustrated by his inability to indict or convict anyone. There was frustration enough to go around. Heth, ordered back to Camp Floyd, blamed the humiliation of the court and the army on the unwillingness of officials in Washington to endorse a sterner policy. "President Buchanan," he observed, "said no blood would be shed during his administration. Brigham Young, who was kept well posted, knew this and acted accordingly."[38]

Heth's frustration still smoldered even with the confrontation ended. Denied the chance to fire at the harassing host of uncivilized Mormons, he wrote two viciously anti-Mormon essays and laced his memoirs with outrage at Young and his Saints.[39]

Yet something came out of the Utah experience that did bring him some satisfaction. Despite the great pressure he faced in Provo, the harassment, the rage of local citizens, his own and his soldiers' dis-

---

37. Ibid., 145; Norman Furness, *The Mormon Conflict, 1850–1859* (New Haven: Yale Univ. Press, 1960), 217–18; Charles P. Roland, *Albert Sidney Johnston: Soldier of Three Republics* (Austin: Univ. of Texas Press, 1964), 223–26.

38. Morrison, *Memoirs of Heth,* 146, xxxviii; Roland, *Albert Sidney Johnston,* 227.

39. Morrison, *Memoirs of Heth,* 107, 146.

gust at the brutality and immorality of the populace, he apparently had done well. "I was much complimented on my return by my superiors and others with my management of affairs while in Provo," he reported. It was his second commendation. The first had followed his successful escape from the Indian camp.

For the second time in his career, he had been officially praised. Both times had seen him threatened — surrounded by a danger more threatening, or at least more ambiguous, than a standing army — but in the face of such danger he had kept his head. The first time he had coolly staged an orderly and apparently unfrightened withdrawal from danger. This time he had balanced restraint again with a show of strength. Dealing with civilians who showed no respect for the flag, little capacity for self-discipline, Heth had known the power of a threat of force.[40]

In 1860 Heth left the West. Given a leave of absence to visit a sick daughter, he journeyed back to Virginia. The farther east he traveled, the more he heard talk of war. He was naturally troubled by it. The impending conflict promised profound decisions for United States soldiers. He was angry at South Carolina hotheads whom he believed were responsible for the crisis. He threatened to help dig up the Palmetto state and thrown it into the sea. When Virginia seceded, however, Heth joined his native state. He felt anguish over resigning after thirteen satisfying years in the blue uniform, but he could do similar work wearing gray.[41]

A phase of his life had ended, one in which he had found great satisfaction and been rewarded with promotions and commendations. He had shown his capacity to balance force with restraint and thus earned a reputation as a responsible officer. He had lived in a world where much of his fate was in his own hands. He had developed a circle of West Point friends to help his career and provide him cordial company. He had shown his mettle in difficult situations and been commended. He had faced the dangerous ambiguities of guerrilla warfare, of civilian-military clashes, and conducted himself well. Heth had learned the necessity of killing but shown himself capable of refraining from killing when the odds of reprisal were high.

40. Ibid., 149-51.
41. Ibid.

In these circumstances he had discovered the superiority of disciplined regulars and learned to admire his own self-control leading
such men. He had been in situations in which he might have lost his
grip but had not. Who could tell why? Perhaps his orders had been
compelling; perhaps the consequences of falling apart were obvious; maybe he had been lucky. Yet the quality of the man himself
and the world he had made surely sustained him. Despite occasional
frustrations, his world had been a simple, ordered one, understand-
able, manipulable — it had human scale. And there was also the
comfort of his own career, with its success to fall back on, to give
him the security from which to make the proper decisions.

From time to time an ominous undercurrent had emerged — a tendency to lash out, to reach for the sword as a solution, to meet defi-
ance with iron — but generally things had worked out well. The
small-scale, relatively simple conflicts of Mexico, Nebraska, Kansas, and Utah had left Heth in control of his fate. Despite the prospective dangers of an onrushing war, it must have been a comfortable feeling to be thirty-five years old and to have such a career to
look back on. It promised good things to come.

As Heth entered combat in 1861, however, things began to un-
ravel. His first duty took him with Brigadier General William Taliaferro to capture the navy yard at Norfolk. The expedition arrived to
find the ships scuttled, the navy yard burned. There was nothing to
capture. The troops marched back empty-handed to Richmond.[42]

Heth's next assignment produced what he recalled as "one of the
most farcical and ridiculous campaigns that occurred during our
war, or any other war." He joined John B. Floyd's campaign in West
Virginia. When another former Virginia governor, Henry Wise, was
also made a general and also given permission to operate in the same
area, the hatred of the two politicians for each other burgeoned.
They spent much of their time working against each other, display-
ing their military incompetence. Heth was kept busy trying to keep
Floyd from getting himself and his troops wiped out or captured.
Frustration and folly, no glory for anybody — these were the prod-
ucts of the time in West Virginia. Once war got out of the hands of
military men, it seemed, such would be the result. Heth had to use
all his thirteen years of military success simply to keep folly from

42. Ibid., 152–56.

turning into disaster. He sought a way out. He began to look forward to being anywhere else. He wrote to fellow Virginian Robert E. Lee to ask for help in getting a transfer. Lee complied and Heth escaped the quicksand.[43]

As 1862 began, Heth's career was still secure, it seemed. Intimations of difficulty had been revealed in the Taliaferro expedition and in the comic opera foolishness of the Floyd-Wise quarreling, but Lee had come to the rescue and Heth was to have the chance to start again somewhere. One possibility was a return to the West. President Jefferson Davis wanted to settle the feuding in the trans-Mississippi department between Sterling Price and Ben McCulloch by putting Heth in command. However, Missouri politicians interfered and blocked this opportunity, and Heth was glad. He had had his fill of bickering politicians and wanted to avoid being mauled in the Price-McCulloch feud.[44]

On January 6, 1862, the thirty-six-year-old Virginian was promoted to brigadier general. There quickly followed a new command: the Lewisburg district of western Virginia. Here was a chance for Heth to get his career moving again and make a name for himself. But the war again began to smother his hope. He was placed in a difficult position—the mountain terrain rose up to defy him. There were few roads in good weather. In bad weather there were none. The Virginia railroad was so burdened with other duties as the war escalated in complexity that he could not get all the supplies he needed. The mountain environment made his cavalry ineffective; lack of forage further diminished his horses' usefulness. He asked Richmond for more soldiers. The answer was an authorization to levy on the local militia—the mountain people of a part of Virginia that would soon help form the loyal Union state of West Virginia.

Not surprisingly, Heth had trouble raising troops from among these people. Furthermore, he also experienced serious problems with the so-called loyal Confederate rangers of the region. Early in the war the Virginia legislature had authorized the creation of local militia groups known as rangers, to secure the region for the Confederacy. It was a move that backfired when these men, allegedly

43. Ibid., 159.
44. Ibid., 154–62.

protectors of the mountain counties, used their recognition by the state as a license to steal and murder. They took assumed Unionists from their homes, tried and convicted them on the spot, and meted out whatever punishment struck their fancy. They were not very discriminating in their victims, however, and Confederate sympathizers in the region soon began to ask for protection from their "protectors."[45]

Confronting the rangers, Heth was dismayed. He recognized that well-organized and controlled militias might be useful troops and in fact was trying to incorporate such groups in his forces. But he saw these men as criminals who were destroying the loyalty he was trying to protect. Perhaps even worse, the rangers were using their official status to avoid regular military service. Heth asked Virginia Governor John Letcher to stop the organization of such groups in the state. When local people in Heth's command increased their outcry against rangers, Heth himself moved to disarm them and bring them under control.[46]

While he was trying to control the rangers, Heth was also organizing regular action. In May 1862 he moved to Giles Courthouse and routed the Federal troops defending the place. Heth's mountain recruits fought as well as his regulars, and the enemy suffered over one hundred casualties. Flushed with success, Heth now marched quickly toward Lewisburg. There approximately 1,500 Federals waited. Heth's numerical superiority, at 2,000 men, the possibility of surprise, and his initiative in the battle all portended another victory, but the result was, in his words, "a signal disaster." "One of those causeless panics for which there is no accounting seized my command," he wrote. "Victory was in my grasp, instead of which I have to admit a most disgraceful defeat."[47]

Heth returned, defeated, to camp. Now the hostility of the mountain region increased its pressure on him. Already tormented by the problem with the rangers, angered by defeat, and frustrated by the impossible logistical position, Heth was pushed to the breaking point by the refusal of local citizens to enlist in his service. Angered, he defied them. On June 9, 1862, he issued a proclamation nullify-

45. *O.R.,* ser. 1, vol. 51, 511, 526, 531; V.C. Jones, *Gray Ghosts and Rebel Raiders,* 26–27.
46. *OR,* ser. 1, vol. 12, pt. 1, 813. Morrison, *Memoirs of Heth,* xxxvii–xxxix.
47. *OR,* ser. 1, vol. 51, 584.

ing all medical exemptions from the service, all exemptions granted
by local authorities. All males between eighteen and thirty-five were
ordered to report for duty immediately. Men who failed to do so
would be "shot as deserters, wherever found."

The proclamation was legally correct. The counties affected had
been placed under martial law by Jefferson Davis. Although it was
not a crime, it was, to use Antoine Boulay's words, worse than a
crime—it was a blunder. In a region where loyalty to the Confederacy had to be carefully nurtured, Heth's heavy-handedness brought
immediate protest to Richmond. The response from the secretary of
war was quick and stinging. Heth's order was rescinded, and he was
transferred to a new command—to Kirby Smith in Chattanooga.[48]

His new assignment only provided more frustration. In the last
half of August 1862, Smith planned an invasion of Kentucky. He
would make a direct move into the Cumberland Gap. Heth was assigned to bring artillery and supplies by another route. Smith
marched victoriously into Barboursville, forcing the Union forces
to retreat. But Heth, unable to move his command very quickly because of poor rail facilities, arrived four days late.[49]

Smith then followed his success with another—on to Richmond,
Kentucky, where he routed another Union force on August 30. Once
again Heth fell afoul of the poor rail system of the region. Again he
arrived too late to be part of this victory. It began to look like Heth's
career was being hounded by failure.

Then the young general hit upon a plan that might put him back
in control again. He went to Kirby Smith with a proposition. He
would follow up the recent victories with the capture of one of the
most important cities in the West, Cincinnati. He pleaded with
Smith for the chance. The commander said he would think it over.
At midnight one evening, Smith told Heth that he could take 6,000
men, several batteries of artillery, and make a "demonstration" toward Cincinnati. Heth leaped at the chance, and the campaign was
a general's dream. He marched twenty-five miles a day and all fell
before him. Only a few skirmishers blocked the way and he swept
them aside disdainfully. Word came from Cincinnati that the city
was in a panic and no organized force was there. Authorities were

48. Ibid.
49. Morrison, *Memoirs of Heth,* xl.

impressing doctors, lawyers, and shopkeepers as soldiers. They were painting tree trunks black to disguise them as cannons. Heth was furnished with a complete inventory of all government supplies and property in the city. The prize would soon be his.[50]

Then on the tenth of September a direct order came from General Smith: no attack was to be made on Cincinnati. Heth was to return to Lexington. Smith told him that Braxton Bragg—soon to meet Don Carlos Buell in "a great battle"—was to be the instrument whereby "Cincinnati and Louisville will fall like ripe apples into our hands." Returning to Smith, Heth could only watch from afar the events that would link another's name with the fall of Cincinnati. There was the possibility of some satisfaction if Bragg could gain the victory, but even this hope was soon crushed. Bragg's erratic behavior snatched humiliation from the jaws of victory and Heth had a ringside seat.

Smith had offered Bragg assistance should he need it in defeating Buell. Bragg rejected the offer and sent a note to the commander bragging that he would meet the Union general alone and "crush him like an eggshell." Smith showed the note to Heth. A short time later a second note came from Bragg that was a 180-degree turn. He dared not fight Buell, Bragg wrote. If he did, his army would be destroyed. Reading the note, Heth was thunderstruck. "Can he be crazy? Has he lost his mind?" Whatever the state of Bragg's mind, he continued to retreat, to refuse to fight. Finally near Perryville he encountered Buell, but without the assistance of Smith, who was too far away to help. When Smith finally got to Perryville, he proposed that they join forces and attack Buell, but Bragg refused. He began plans to withdraw from Kentucky. There would be no victory. There would be no Cincinnati or Louisville for Heth, not even a shared victory. In late October 1862 the Gray army passed back through the Cumberland Gap, back into Tennessee.[51]

Meanwhile, as the army suffered the frustrations of this campaign, Heth's career received another rebuke. In October the Confederate senate got Jefferson Davis's list of recommended promotions. Heth was listed for major general, but the committee on military affairs recommended against his promotion. The senate, without debate,

50. Ibid., 165–66.
51. Ibid., 166–67; Thomas Connelly, *Autumn of Glory* (Baton Rouge: LSU Press, 1971), 105–08.

agreed. Heth got the message. He saw little hope for advancement where he was. Maybe another change of commands would help. He wrote President Davis to ask for assignment to Robert E. Lee and the Army of Northern Virginia. "General Lee has always been my personal friend," Heth wrote in November, "and I should like to join him for many reasons." Lee, taking what one historian calls, "an unusual personal interest in Heth's career," wrote Richmond in support of Heth's request.[52]

While Heth was casting about for a place where he might put his career back in order, he took command of East Tennessee as Kirby Smith moved into Middle Tennessee. The East Tennessee command was in a continuing state of confusion. In less than a year nine men had held it and then moved on. It was hardly a promising spot for Heth, for it harbored the bitter Appalachian guerrilla war seething with treacherous ambiguities like those he had faced at Lewisburg. It was a place where brutality was constant and the enemy too often a ghost. It was a command where a politically insensitive leader, one stung by recent defeats and missed opportunities, a man fearing mortal wounds to his lifelong career and at an age where personal mortality begins to scratch for attention, a man longing to rush away to the protection of a powerful and revered friend might be tempted to do something brutal, or to order it done, or perhaps out of weariness or calculated carelessness, allow it to happen.[53]

52. Morrison, *Memoirs of Heth,* xli, lxxi.
53. Connelly, *Autumn of Glory,* 107.

LOYALTY
AND TREASON
IN THE
MOUNTAINS

Men or squads of men, who commit hostilities, whether by fighting or inroads for destruction or plunder or by raids of any kind without commission, without being part and portion of the organized hostile army, and without sharing continuously in the war, but who do so with intermitting returns to their homes and avocations, or with the occasional assumption of the semblance of peaceful pursuits, divesting themselves of the character of appearance of soldiers—such men, or squads of men, are not public enemies, and therefore, if captured, are not entitled to the privileges of prisoners of war, but shall be treated summarily as highway robbers or pirates.

Instructions for the Government of Armies of the United States in the Field (1863) Article LXXXII, "General Orders 100,"

The brutal ambiguities that Heth faced in the embattled mountains had been revealed as soon as the secession crisis began. The Appalachian counties of Tennessee and North Carolina, like others throughout the South, were bitterly divided, and the division was not just ideological, not just over the theory of union or disunion. The line was often drawn between rich and poor. Upper classes tended to support secession. They organized to make sure that votes on disunion went the right way. Wealth and social position were easily translated into political and legal power. People of wealth were the sheriffs, the county clerks, and the court judges. Furthermore, being concentrated in the cities, they could organize more easily than could their opponents. Consequently, Unionists faced tough going in the secession crisis, especially at the polls.[1]

Throughout the mountains the elections for delegates to the secession conventions in 1861 took place in an atmosphere of tension and imminent violence. In Henderson County, North Carolina, armed men came to the ballot boxes. Clerks stood by taking the names of all those who voted for "the Lincoln candidate." Threats were shouted that such traitors would be hanged or shot. Boys of fifteen and sixteen were sent to vote for secession. Union voters were often intimidated into not voting at all. This coercion was so effective that the number of votes in the region was down 46,000 from previous tallies.[2]

Madison County was perhaps the most bitterly divided of all the Tarheel state's mountain counties, and an incident during the May 1861 convention election was indicative of the character of this division. As was usual on election day throughout most of the nation, the bars were open to help voters celebrate or lament their party's future. The county sheriff had been making the rounds of Marshall during the day and by early afternoon was full of enthusiasm for the secessionist cause. Standing on Main Street, he began to shout the virtues of Jefferson Davis and other Rebel patriots. A crowd gathered round. Taking inspiration, a Unionist replied with a shout for George Washington and the Union. The sheriff whipped out his pistol and advanced toward the Unionist, who began to back away. A cooler and clearer header stranger intervened, and the sheriff turned his attention to another voter who was at the ballot box.

"Why did you bring your gun with you?" the sheriff demanded. The man's answer did not satisfy him and so out came the pistol again. The voter backed away and the crowd began to duck for cover. The sheriff, now obviously feeling besieged by traitors, spotted another of this breed in the crowd—this time a fellow he had quarreled with before. The sheriff advanced, pistol drawn. The intended victim jumped behind some bystanders, but the sheriff fired anyway and the bullet struck the man's son.

The scene had stopped being funny and was becoming deadly.

---

1. Thomas William Humes, *The Loyal Mountaineers of Tennessee* (Knoxville, Tenn.: Ogden Bros., 1888), 91, 97; Dykeman, *The French Broad*, 80–81.
2. Alexander H. Jones, *Knocking at the Door* (Washington, D.C.: McGill & Witherow, 1866), 5.

The sheriff looked for cover and found it in a nearby house. The owner, fearing that the angry crowd outside might storm into his home, slammed the door, and the sheriff rushed upstairs, threw open a second story window, and defied the "damned black Republicans" to shoot it out with him. The father of the bleeding boy accepted the challenge. He fired and wounded the sheriff seriously. The town constable then moved to get control of things and rushed to the house. He took the sheriff into custody, but the father wanted more immediate justice. Dashing in behind the constable, he fired a second shot that killed the wounded man. In the turmoil that followed, the killer escaped into the mountains. Later he joined the Union army in Kentucky and died in the war. Feelings ran so high, however, that after the war the sheriff's descendants filed suit against seven men whom they accused of aiding the killer.[3]

Incidents like this arose from the deep division of loyalties in the southern highlands. In the presidential election of 1860 southern candidates John Bell and John Cabell Breckinridge divided the North Carolina mountain counties between them ten to ten. The electoral picture from Madison that year was so confusing and suspect that the returns were thrown out. In 1861 the county voted on two issues — should there be a convention to act on secession and who should Madison's delegate be. Conforming to statewide results, the county went 532–345 against a convention and chose a Unionist delegate. The closeness of the vote, however, showed that loyalties were divided in Madison. The postwar picture would be the same. In 1868 only seventy-one votes separated the Democrats and the victorious Republicans. Whereas voting statistics reflect degrees of commitment to parties and causes, there are other figures that reflect the passion of Unionist sentiment in Madison and surrounding counties.[4]

Unionist mountaineers cast their whole vote for their beliefs. From a region surrounded by Confederate territory came two mounted North Carolina regiments to fight for the Union cause. Hundreds of men joined Tennessee, Kentucky, and other northern regiments, and Union recruiters roamed the area with considerable

3. Dykeman, *French Broad,* 128–31.
4. Salisbury *Carolina Watchman,* Dec. 4, 1860, March 25, 1861; McKinney, *Southern Mountain Republicans,* 16–17; Walter Burnham, *Presidential Ballots* (Baltimore: John Hopkins Univ. Press, 1955), 659.

success. Alexander Jones, Unionist congressman from Henderson County, estimated that from the twenty-one western counties of the Tarheel state 5,790 men escaped to Union lines and three-quarters of them joined the Union army.[5]

Unionist sentiment in Madison and other mountain counties grew from several roots, none of which was apparently strong enough alone to produce the result but which combined were sufficient. The source most often mentioned both by modern historians and the descendants of Unionists is the region's lack of involvement with slavery. "Our people being mountain folks," Glendora Cutchell wrote, "had poor land, [and] did not own slaves. . . . Therefore their sympathy was with the Union." Certainly the involvement of Madison's highlanders with slavery was slight. Whereas North Carolina had 35,000 slaveholders as of 1860, the county had 46. The state had over 330,000 slaves, but Madison County had 213.[6]

The relative absence of slavery, however, did not make the mountain people abolitionists. Knoxville editor William G. Brownlow pointed out in May of 1861 that if the newly established Lincoln government moved against slavery, "there would not be a Union man among us in twenty four hours." Like many northerners, Unionist highlanders disliked Negroes as well as slavery, an attitude epitomized by Andrew Johnson and destructive of postwar support for Republican policies. Furthermore, they shared resentment of outside interference with their racial prejudices.[7]

Their Unionism was not founded on racial egalitarianism but a resentment of slaveholders, a resentment that in many cases took on class lines. Slaveholders in the mountains tended to be wealthier than their neighbors. They were, as Olmsted noted, "chiefly professional men, shopkeepers, and men in office, who are also land owners and give a divided attention to farming." They were, in short, men with ties to the state governments, to the world outside the mountains, and to the slave-dominated southern economy. As the rural mountaineers became more and more isolated, as increas-

5. William Cotton, "Appalachian North Carolina" (Ph.D. diss., Univ. of North Carolina, 1954), 126; A. H. Jones, *Knocking at the Door,* passim; William Burson, *Race for Liberty* (Wellsville, Ohio: W.G. Foster, 1867).
   6. U.S. Census, 1860, *Population,* 209–10; Cutchell, "First Sheltons", 2.
   7. *Knoxville Whig,* May 18, 1861; Allen Trelease, "Who Were the Scalawags?" *Journal of Southern History* 29 (1963), 445–68.

ing family size diminished individual wealth, reasons grew for re-
senting beneficiaries of the southern system.[8]

Heritage also contributed to Unionism. Many parts of the mountain region were settled originally by northern immigrants who
moved down the valleys of Appalachia. Places like Shelton Laurel
that were settled from Virginia also retained memories likely to foster nationalism. Two of the first settlers in Shelton Laurel, Roderick
and William Shelton, had fought for American independence. Like
others of their kin, they had moved to the valley shortly after that
war, and the increasing isolation and the kinship of the people in
Shelton Laurel made it unlikely that they would be attracted to the
growing disunion sentiment of the South. The strength of such historical experiences was well understood by mountain Unionist politicians like Andrew Johnson. His speeches against secession were
filled with historical references and calls to the traditions of the
nation-making years.[9]

Johnson's private correspondence also suggested the basis for
Unionism in class and how class might be linked with history to produce supporters of Lincoln and the North. After Johnson made his
famous speeches of the secession winter attacking southern disunion, his East Tennessee constituents responded. Dozens of letters
came to him from poor and almost illiterate people, described as
"the mountain boys—the wood choppers—the rail splitters—in fact
the bone and sinew of the country . . . entirely irrespective of party."
A carpenter from Hawkins County wrote, "What I want to aske of
you is if you please Send me your Speaches I hav Nevere Seen Enny
of them yet I Liv in Sitch a out of the way place that we poore folks
is Never thought of I have tolde my Neighbours (all of them for
you) that I would write to you and aske you to think of me and that
would do for all they is nothing talk of But your union Speach and it
has made you more friends than Enny thing you evere did."

Unionists insisted that secessionists in the mountains were wealthy
office holders and men of private influence, and when Johnson attacked his enemies and the South, he accused them of being "mon-

8. Olmsted, *A Journey in the Back Country,* 226; Humes, *Loyal Mountaineers,*
91, 97; Dykeman, *French Broad,* 80–81; Cotton, "Appalachian North Carolina", 94.

9. Cutchell, "First Sheltons"; Andrew Johnson, "Speech on Secession," in *The
Papers of Andrew Johnson,* vol. 4, ed. LeRoy Graf and Ralph Haskins (Knoxville:
Univ. of Tennessee Press, 1976), 3–15.

archists" who wanted to enslave the independent common people. By contrast, his people in East Tennessee were "homogeneous, industrious, frugal . . . independent, but harmless and powerless . . . rode over by usurpers." These ambitious tyrants would fail, he claimed; "they will never take us out of this Union, or make us a land of slaves — no, never. We intend to stand as firm, as adamant, and as unyielding as our own majestic mountains." "The hardy mountaineers," as a correspondent called them, were ready to oppose disunion tyranny.[10]

Other mountain Unionist politicians played the theme of common, hard-working, independent mountain people fighting a disunion aristocracy. North Carolina's Alexander Jones accused his state's disunionists of being slavocrats who "look upon a white man who has to labor for an honest living as no better than one of their negroes. . . . these bombastic, high falutin, aristocratic fools have been in the habit of driving negroes and poor helpless white people until they think they can control the world of mankind." William Brownlow, editor of *The Knoxville Whig and Rebel Ventilator,* insisted that the distinction between Union and disunion men was that Unionists did "not think it *degrading* to a man to labor, as do most of the Southern Disunionists."[11]

Without doubt there were wealthy men who supported the Union cause. For example, while Brownlow declared that he was a poor man, in the same sentence he claimed to be worth about $10,000. Neither Andrew Johnson nor Alexander Jones was poor in comparison with his constituents, and Unionists held government offices too. Nevertheless, the evidence is strong to suggest that in the mountains wealth, especially wealth in slaves, was correlated with support for the Confederacy and office holding was likely to indicate disunion sentiment.[12]

Mountain Unionism thus interwove class hostility, rural suspicions of more urban places, and a feeling that the wealthy and influential slave owners were threatening hard-working common people.

10. *Papers of Andrew Johnson,* vol. 4, 166, 189–90, 360, 417, 618–23, 639, 694.
11. A.H. Jones, *Knocking at the Door,* 6–16; W.G. Brownlow, *Sketches of the Rise, Progress and Decline of Secession* (Philadelphia: n.p., 1862), 17, 49–50, 88.
12. Brownlow, *Sketches of Secession,* 17. Cotton, in "Appalachian North Carolina," notes that in the North Carolina secession convention, Unionists argued for popular ratification of the secession resolution and for equal taxation on slaves as well as land. Secessionists defeated both measures by 2 to 1. See 84–87.

Such sentiments would later surface throughout North Carolina, though predominantly in the western half, in the accusation that the conflict was "a rich man's war and a poor man's fight." Visiting the state shortly after Appomattox, Sidney Andrews observed that much of "the Unionism of Western North Carolina of which we heard so much during the war . . . was less a love for the Union than a personal hatred of those who went into the Rebellion. It was not so much an uprising for the government as against a certain ruling class."[13]

Of course, local feelings and experiences shaped loyalties too. As the mountaineers became more isolated from the outside world, they became more isolated from one another. Quarrels between neighborhoods, family antagonisms, long brooding on real and imagined insults, helped mold decisions of whom to fight for or against. Although the feuding associated with the mountains was apparently a post-Civil War phenomenon, by the beginning of the conflict there seem to have been conditions out of which such antagonism might grow.[14]

Thus the hostility of the mountaineers toward slaveholders and a system that benefited them in no clear way, the growing isolation and poverty of the mountains, and also family and neighborhood traditions and personal antagonisms laid the groundwork for Unionist feelings and sent soldiers to the Union lines. In the early days of the war, hundreds of men tried to get to Union regions in Kentucky to enlist in Lincoln's forces. More often than not, they left their families behind, for the journey was a dangerous one and demanded stealth and the ability to move fast and often risk capture and maybe death.

Although hundreds moved north, most of the mountaineers stayed in the valleys in which they had been born and raised. Many were trapped inside the Confederacy and had little choice. Most would try to avoid service to one side or the other; they would try to live on and hope that their steep ridges would hold back the tides of war. Out of this population, however, it was easy to raise armed men to prey upon the Confederates. The advantages of such service to

13. Sidney Andrews, *The South Since the War* (Boston: Ticknor & Fields, 1866), 111–12; Cotton, "Appalachian North Carolina," 124–28.

14. Cratis Williams, "The Southern Mountaineer in Fact and Fiction," *Appalachian Journal* 3 (1975), 25.

these men were clear. They could fight when it suited them and yet comfort themselves with the thought that they were protecting the "Grand Ole Flag" and the "Union of their Fathers." They could foray quickly against Rebel railroads, bridges, and supplies and then vanish swiftly into the security of the mountains and return to the comforts of home. There was none of the endless boredom of regular service in faraway camps. No strangers to order a man about. No fighting in terrain chosen by some fancy pants officers. No death in some unknown field or a nameless grave far away from home, friends, and family. No constant worry about the survival and comfort of those at home while one served helplessly hundreds of miles away. This sort of fighting had its advantages. A man could stay in the mountain valley he loved. It seemed that he could almost choose when and where the war would happen to him.

This is not to say that the men of the mountains were all loyalists. The promises of quick victory, the slogans proclaiming secession as salvation from centralized coercion, the excitement of the moment, the glory of protecting home, family, and friends from Lincoln and his black Republicans — these inspired enlistments in the armies of the gray. By the end of 1861 nearly 9,000 North Carolina mountaineers had become Confederate soldiers. From 800 to 1,000 men from Madison County served in the Sixty-four North Carolina Infantry Regiment, and still others served in other regiments. The county was not pure Unionist. It did not deserve the name given to Wilkes County of "the Old United States."[15]

Among the Confederate loyalists were many poor people. The charge that Lincoln's govenment intended to unleash a racial revolution in the South was ceaseless. Poor whites, profoundly hostile to blacks and most vulnerable to any change in the social and economic structure, accepted disunion declarations of independence for racial purity's sake. One thing that distinguished poor supporters of disunion from poor Unionists may have been that the latter owned some land and were further away from the slave population. Slaves and free blacks were much more prevalent closer to moun-

---

15. Albert D. Richardson, *The Secret Service, the Field, the Dungeon, and the Escape* (Hartford, American Pub. Co., 1865), 451; J. W. Moore, *Roster of North Carolina Troops in the War Between the States,* vol. 4 (Raleigh, N.C.: Ashe, 1882), 50–81; Cotton, "Appalachian North Carolina," 88; Barrett, *Civil War in North Carolina,* 181–82.

tain cities and towns than in the hinterlands. Urban votes for secession may have come from the poor as well as the influential.[16]

There were more immediate reasons for support of the Confederacy among the poorer portions of society. Because of the influence of secessionists, it was wise to decide that one's sympathies lay with the South. Faced with the presence of Confederate power and the lack of armed organized Federal protection, reasonable men not seeking martyrdom might become southern patriots. For many among all classes there was little pleasure in being citizens of the new republic. One North Carolina woman expressed her sorrow to a friend: "The Union is gone and all these things follow it, as the shadow steals after a great strong man who goes out from your door forever! How quietly we drift out into such an awful night into the darkness, the lowering clouds, the howling winds, and the ghostly light of our former glory going with us, 'to make the gloom visible' with its pale glare." In such an environment it is not surprising that devotion to the Confederate cause was often not very deep.[17]

Men who swore their loyalty to Dixie often swore, as one fellow put it, "from the teeth out." Others, discovering that the war would be long and brutal, determined that they were better off at home. Others had been coerced into enlisting in the first place and took the first opportunity to desert and return to their mountains. Whatever the reasons were that brought these early Rebel enlistees back, they soon became plentiful in the region and their numbers would swell as the war continued.

This disloyalty worried Confederates from the early days of the war, and with good reason. Lincoln himself was trying to use mountain Unionists to attack the Confederacy. He chose Samuel Carter of the navy to organize regular army units in East Tennessee. His brother, William Carter, brought Sam a plan he had devised during September to disrupt the railroad traffic between Bristol, Virginia, and Stevenson, Alabama, by destroying the nine railroad bridges of the railroad. The destruction of the bridges would damage the transport of supplies from the upper to the lower Confederacy. Lieutenant Carter sent the plan to Lincoln, who endorsed it and provided $1,000 pay for the raids.

16. Cotton, "Appalachian North Carolina," 88–90; Williams, "Southern Mountaineer in Fact and Fiction," 24–25.
17. Quoted in McKinney, *Southern Mountain Republicans,* 19.

On November 8, 1861, the raid began. Five of the bridges were burned but the other four were saved. Confederate authorities quickly moved troops to the area. Martial law was declared. Hundreds of Unionists, called Tories by their captors, were taken prisoner and several of the suspected bridge burners were hanged. The Rebel government believed that an example should be made of the consequences of this treason, and so the War Department in Richmond ordered that the bodies of the Tories be left hanging from trees near the bridges they had burned. This provided some sport for passengers along the route near Greeneville, Tennessee, who reportedly reached out from passing trains and beat the bodies as they moved by.

Not all the bridge burners were taken, however. While many of the captured men suffered this fate, some were successful. At Lick Creek in Greene County, Tennessee, Union Colonel David Fry inaugurated a short career that would make him one of the region's most-wanted men. Although guards had been posted at the Lick Creek bridge, Fry and his men surprised and overwhelmed them. Not content just to burn the bridges, Fry abused and cursed the captured guards, taunting them as traitors, while his soldiers burned the bridge. Escaping from Confederate reinforcements, Fry moved down the line between Chattanooga and Marietta, Georgia, stealing locomotives, destroying tracks, and cutting telegraph lines.[18]

In the eyes of Confederate authorities, these were not isolated incidents. They were signs of a potential levy en masse throughout the mountains that could prepare the way for a Union invasion. Jefferson Davis heard in November 1861 that Unionists along the North Carolina line "look confidently for the re-establishment of the federal authority in the South with as much confidence as the Jews look for the coming of the Messiah. . . . no event or circumstance can change or modify their hopes." In the presence of Confederate forces, another Rebel wrote, the Unionists were ready to swear allegiance, but once troops left the area this loyalty died. Worse from the Confederate viewpoint was the fact that the Unionists were militant opponents of secession. "Whenever a foreign force enters this country, be it soon or late, three-fourths of this people will rise in

18. *OR,* ser. 1, vol. 10, 636–37; ser. 2, vol. 1, 862–64; Albert Castel, "The Guerrilla War," Special Issue of *Civil War Times Illustrated,* Oct. 1974.

arms to join them," Colonel D. Ledbetter wrote from Greenville, Tennessee.[19]

Suspicions of mountain loyalty continued through the spring of 1862 and then were felt in an environment of impending Union attack. In the fall of 1861, General Grant had gained control of the mouth of the Cumberland and Tennessee rivers. Then in January 1862 the Federal armies, over 100,000 strong and facing a force of about half that size, began to move through Kentucky and toward Tennessee. Mill Springs in Kentucky fell on the nineteenth. On February 6 Union forces captured Fort Henry, six days later Fort Donaldson fell, and the defense of Nashville began to collapse. General Albert Sidney Johnston's army fell back to the Tennessee-Mississippi border to regroup, and Grant moved forward. By March 1862 Kirby Smith, commanding the Department of East Tennessee, saw danger from the rear as well as the front. The region was "an enemy's country. The people are against us, and ready to rise whenever an enemy's column makes its appearance. The very troops raised here cannot always be depended upon. They have gone into service, many of them to escape suspicion, prepared to give information to the enemy, and ready to pass over to him when an opportunity arises." Smith asked for a declaration of martial law throughout his district. Recent state elections in Tennessee had resulted in victories for open supporters of the Federal government. Hoping to counteract the possible consequences, Smith secretly dispatched squads of twenty-five men to the county seats to present loyalty oaths to the newly elected officers. If the oaths were refused, the men were to be arrested.[20]

Then, in the aftermath of the Union victory at Shiloh on April 7, 1862, President Davis gave Smith the declaration of martial law he had asked for. Civil jurisdiction in the Department of East Tennessee was suspended except for property transfers and the assessment of county taxes. The privilege of the writ of *habeas corpus* was suspended. Furthermore, Smith was given the power to organize a military policy to enforce a new order prohibiting "the distillation of spiritous liquors." Smith moved to balance the severity of military authority by offering amnesty to those persons who took a loyalty

19. *OR,* ser. 2, vol. 1, 841–49.
20. *OR,* ser. 1, vol. 10, pt. 2, 320, 385–87.

oath to the Confederacy and who returned to Confederate territory after having tried to escape to Union lines. Furthermore, Smith promised, property rights would be respected in his command, and he would suspend the militia draft during the growing season, but any men who left the area to escape to the Federal forces would have their families thrown off the land and sent after them. These efforts to weaken the Unionism of the mountaineers, however, brought little success. Although the presence of Confederate soldiers could generate statements of loyalty, opportunities to support the Union cause called forth much more loudly heard behavior.[21]

Some of the most startling came from David Fry, of Lick Creek bridge fame. The Union officer roamed the mountain regions throughout the winter of 1862, threatening the Confederate population and "confiscating" their money, weapons, and provisions. He also sought to recruit men into Federal service. Since he often stayed in Shelton Laurel between his raids, it was natural that he would find enlistees among the men there, and several joined him. He told them that they would try to get to Union lines in Kentucky, where their enlistments would be formalized. When the group tried to get to Kentucky, however, there were too many Confederate troops blocking the passes and Fry had them return to their homes. They would try again.[22]

Meanwhile the Confederates tired of Fry's depredations, and in early 1862 a contingent of soldiers came after him. Fry heard of the impending attack, gathered together nineteen men, and set out for Kentucky and safety. The small detachment never made it. They were captured and sent to Atlanta prison. Then the authorities moved to punish the valley that had sheltered Fry.

On April 7, 1862, a detachment of the Forty-third Tennessee Regiment moved from Greeneville toward Shelton Laurel. The valley there was known as "a general resort and hiding place for outlaws," and their orders were to "put down any illegal organization of men that might be found there." It was a difficult assignment because the

21. Ibid., 402-403, 640-41; Ella Lonn, *Desertion During the Civil War* (New York: Century, 1928), 49.

22. *Report of the Committee on Pensions*, #44, 43d Cong., 1st sess., Serial Set 1586. There were similar cases throughout the region where enlistments into the Union army were rather casual. After the war pension claims rested on the question of whether or not the enlistee had in fact served with an organized unit. See Serial Sets 1409, Rept. 195; 1548, Rept. 466; 1576, Rept. 15.

terrain favored the outlaws. The sides of the valley were often steep, and laurel bushes covered these walls so densely that a man sometimes could not stand up as he moved through the thicket. Locals had a saying that in these mountains a person could shoot a squirrel fifty feet away and have to walk a mile to fetch it.

Lieutenant Colonel Key, commanding the detachment, tried to protect his column by spreading out scouts on either side of the line of march, but this brought the men little real safety. Throughout the eighth, ninth, and tenth of April the soldiers continued their hunt. No regular force challenged them. Instead, snipers in groups of four to ten fired from hiding. When the soldiers grouped to storm their assailants, the snipers quickly retreated into the forest. Three long and frustrating days apparently did bring some success, however. Key reported to his superiors a "body count" of fifteen enemy dead. Only three casualties were reported among the regulars. Key believed, however, that the region was still in enemy hands, that every man there who could bear a gun would use it against the Confederacy, and that the rest of the population would support them.[23]

A few days later the Confederates struck again, and this time they had more to cheer about. General Marcus Erwin, commanding the state militia, with a much larger force than Key had headed, blocked all the passes leading in and out of the valley and systematically moved through it, arresting between thirty and forty ringleaders and convincing others of the benefits of joining the Confederate army. Then Erwin left. Shortly thereafter, Unionist bands operating out of the Shelton Laurel region were reported to be engaged in raids into East Tennessee.[24]

Raids by Confederate soldiers were not the only threats to the people of Shelton Laurel. Even as Erwin's troops marched away, events unfolded that would make the war more than just an occasional intruder. On April 16, 1862, the Confederate congress passed the new nation's first draft law. The first surge of enthusiasm that had swelled the gray ranks was subsiding, and compulsion was needed to sustain the fight for independence. All able-bodied men eighteen to thirty-five years old were made eligible for conscription

23. *OR,* ser. 1, vol. 1, 628–29; Cotton, "Appalachian North Carolina," 95–97, 147.

24. Cotton, "Appalachian North Carolina," 21, 147. J.V. Hadley, *Seven Months a Prisoner* (New York: Scribner's, 1898), 180–81.

by the Confederate government. There were a few exemptions, of course. Most government officials, state and national, were ex-empt, as were workers in the iron industry, the railroads and other forms of transportation, most printers, college teachers and presi-dents, teachers of more than twenty students, supervisors and nurses in health services (but not doctors), one apothecary per apothecary shop, and those workers in wool and cotton factories designated by the secretary of war. The law also allowed men to pay substitutes to serve in their place. None of these exemptions offered relief to more than a small fraction of the people of western North Carolina. To rural mountain people they offered none.[25]

What the draft did produce was a changed environment for the pro-Unionist mountaineers of Madison County. First of all, it alien-ated earlier supporters of the Confederate cause. The large numbers of young men from the mountains who had joined the army in 1861 were predominantly the farmers of the region. The prospect of hav-ing more men taken away raised the specter of food shortages. Who would plant and harvest if the farmers were at war? Having volun-tarily given so much to the cause, many mountain people resented facing deprivation due to the coercion of the government. The only two votes in the lower house of the Confederate congress against the draft bill came from representatives of western North Carolina. Here were signs to encourage boldness from mountain Unionists. Here also was reason to increase the fears and the anxieties of loyal rebels in and outside the mountains and perhaps to lead them to des-perate countermeasures.

Conscription also threw new light on the purposes for which the Confederacy fought. Fighting for the right to be left alone was a cause mountaineers could rally around. Being compelled to fight for that right — well, a man did not have to be very sophisticated to smell something wrong with that.[26]

Conscription helped to cause desertion. The draft might force men into the army, but it could not keep them there, and nowhere was this more true than in the mountains. Speaking for thousands,

25. Barrett, *Civil War in North Carolina*, 183–85; Memory Mitchell, *Legal Aspects of Conscription and Exemption in North Carolina, 1861–1865*, (Chapel Hill: Univ. of North Carolina Press, 1965), 11–17; Albert Moore, *Conscription and Conflict in the Confederacy* (New York: Macmillan, 1934), 12–26.
26. Moore, *Conscription and Conflict*, 12–26.

Norman Harrold of Ashe County sent a letter to Jefferson Davis, "bastard president of a political abortion," bidding farewell to "scalp hunters . . . and chivalrous Confederates in crime." "Except it be in the army of the Union," he declared, "you will not again see the conscript."[27]

Nevertheless, there were in the mountains loyal Confederates whose devotion to the cause endured and perhaps was intensified by the peril that spawned conscription. They were determined to hunt down men who in time of need deserted their country, who abandoned those soldiers already in the field. They were ready to hunt deserters wherever they ran, back into the most remote mountain valleys if necessary. Desertion had to be stopped.

The problem of desertion from the rebel cause existed throughout the Confederacy, of course, however much the most virulent form of the disease may have flourished in the mountain region. As early as February 1862, General S.B. Buckner was reporting that three hundred of his men had deserted and were on their way to Henderson, Tennessee. By December of that year the Army of the Tennessee discovered that several thousand men were absent, some of them officers. The Confederate War Department estimated in July 1863 that 50,000 men were AWOL, and the number might, in fact, have neared 100,000. Action to stop desertion took many forms — from shooting to legislation, from appeals to patriotism, and even by subtle sexual threat. Reversing the role of Lysistrata, an unidentified group of southern ladies placed the following plea in several southern newspapers. "It is impossible for us to respect a coward and every true woman who has husband, father, brother, or lover . . . had rather see him prostrate before her with death's signet in his noble brow that has never been branded by cowardice or dishonor, than have him forfeit his good name and disgrace his manhood by refusing to do his duty to his country."[28]

Within the Confederacy, North Carolina led all the rest in desertions. An estimated 24,000 men and officers from the state deserted. Tennessee Volunteers came in second in desertion rankings. Over 12,000 volunteered not to remain in rebel ranks. East Tennessee and western North Carolina housed most of the deserters. By

27. Ibid., 19–21.
28. Lonn, *Desertion During the Civil War,* 49.

late 1862 desertion in Yadkin and Wilkes counties in the Tarheel state had become well organized enough to threaten the elections there, and Confederate troops had to be sent to preserve order. By early 1863 Governor Zeb Vance estimated that there were at least twelve hundred deserters hiding in the western mountains. In Henderson and Cherokee counties there were so many that they practically controlled the counties. Confederate troops might roam throughout the region seeking deserters during the day, but at night the place belonged to the fugitives. In Caldwell County a Confederate captain named Estes described his job as chasing down deserters. "I do this in the daytime and at night I am generally with the boys. Of course, they know enough to keep out of my sight during the day, which makes it exceedingly difficult for me to catch them."[29]

On January 26, 1863, Vance issued a proclamation appealing to deserters to return to their units. Although these men would lose their pay for the period of absence, they would not sacrifice their lives. Full amnesty would be given them. He appealed to the pride they should have in their infant nation and dangled before them the prospect of rewards to be showered on loyal and brave soldiers. Suggesting the steel in his pleas, Vance had asked the North Carolina General Assembly on January 21 for a law making it a crime to harbor deserters.[30]

While deserters and Unionists shaded the mountain region with a coat of blue, enough gray remained to make this region bitterly contested. It was a place filled with danger to strangers who wandered there ignorant of the personal sentiments of those they met or who were unfortunate enough to take the wrong road or wander into the wrong valley. In Lee County, Virginia, in the Cumberland Mountain foothills near Powell River, there was a vigorous group of rebels who boasted they would take no prisoners should they encounter Unionists. Those captured would be killed on the spot. In Johnson County, Kentucky, sometime in January 1863 a Rebel regiment and a contingent of the home guard captured five Unionists. Two of the captives were killed while being taken. The other three were escorted to a tree and strung up. Care was taken not to break their

29. James Madison Drake, *Fast and Loose in Dixie* (New York: Authors Publishing Co., 1887), 176–77.
30. Cotton, "Appalachian North Carolina," 131; Lonn, *Desertion During the Civil War,* 24–30; *OR,* ser. 1, vol. 7, 864.

necks but rather to make sure that they died slowly. As they stran-
gled to death, some of their captors beat them with sticks and guns.
One of the Rebels danced around them and twirled their suspended
bodies.[31]

When Unionists were caught and hanged, their bodies were sometimes left dangling from the trees as a lesson to those who might
consider betraying the Confederate cause. Dan Ellis, a Unionist
who guided hundreds of men through the mountains and into
Union lines, one day discovered three skeletons still hanging from a
branch near a spring. Much of the flesh had rotted off, and the
bones dangled frighteningly in the wind. As he turned to leave, he
met a woman coming down the road. "Why were those men killed?"
he asked her.

She replied, "They were a parcel of Lincolnites that our boys captured at that spring while they were getting water."

"That is a horrible sight, madam. Is that the way that the Lincolnites are disposed of when they are so unfortunate as to be captured?"

"Yes; they receive no mercy whatever from our boys. If you will
go down the road about one hundred yards you will find a parcel of
them that were captured here a short time ago, and were shot immediately, and were thrown behind an old log, and covered up with
leaves and chunks."

"How does it happen that so many men are captured in this neighborhood?"

"Why, there is a company of soldiers stationed on Clinch River,
and they have selected the best hunters in the country to watch the
roads and mountain paths to catch men who are making their way
through the lines."

"Well, that is the most diabolical sight that I have ever witnessed
in my life."

"Oh, that is not a strange sight to me, by any means. I have seen
the hat and shoes taken off of many Lincolnites, and have seen
them kneel to pray before being shot."

"And did it cause you no emotions of pity to witness such a spec-
tacle?"

"No, none whatever. That is the very way that men ought to be

31. *Thrilling Adventures of Daniel Ellis, The Great Union Guide of East Tennessee for a Period of Nearly Four Years During the Great Southern Rebellion. Written
by Himself* (New York: Harper, 1867), 97, 105-10.

treated whenever they are caught running away to Old Abe. All of them ought to be killed."

"But do you think that the poor men whom you have seen murdered so unceremoniously were really guilty of any crime for which they deserved to be killed?"

"Yes, I have no sympathy for them whatever. I believe it is perfectly right to kill them whenever they are caught. I have a husband and two brothers in the Southern army, and every man who is unwilling to fight for the Southern Confederacy, who may be caught in the act of running off to Kentucky, ought to be hung or shot."[32]

Most deserters escaped, and most were not intimidated by such brutality. They combined with the Unionists of the mountains to produce a population loyal to the Union and willing to assist those who sought help. Federal soldiers escaping from prisons in South Carolina, in Georgia, or from the prison in Salisbury, North Carolina, soon heard that safety and help awaited those who could make it to the mountains of North Carolina and East Tennessee. (The existence of pro-Confederate mountaineers was apparently not widely known.) At first the path to freedom was sustained by slaves and free Negroes around the prisons and in the piedmont. Escapees uniformly reported that a hungry man, a man lost and suffering from exposure to the elements, would find food, shelter, and directions to the next safe resting place from any black person he could find. Those who suffered from the bondage of their race quickly aided those who were escaping to freedom themselves, especially when most of them promised to rejoin their units and continue the fight against the Confederacy.

The problem was that this black road to safety and home gradually faded away as a fugitive went west and north. Increasingly the population was white, and the badge of loyalty was no longer painted on the faces of potential friends. Yet as the fugitives moved northwest toward freedom, they found more and more whites willing to help. They discovered that large houses and towns were to be avoided but small cabins were frequently places of rest.

J.V. Hadley and two companions escaped from Andersonville in Georgia and finally made their way into the North Carolina mountains near Hendersonville. There they were spotted by Rebel sol-

32. Ibid., 187–88.

diers and had to scramble up a mountainside and into a thicket of laurels. They lost their pursuers, but the weather was bitterly cold and there was nothing to eat. They dared not make a fire or they would give themselves away. Finally, desperate with cold and hunger, they decided to risk discovery and made their way to a cabbage patch nearby. While Hadley was grabbing cabbages, three young women spotted him. Fearing that they would run to get Rebel soldiers, he tried to keep them from leaving.

"Hallo, girls," he called. "Don't be frightened—we won't hurt you."

"Who are you?" they inquired.

"We are soldiers."

"What kind of soldiers?"

"Confederate soldiers, of course."

"Well, you ought to be engaged in better business."

"What better business can we be at?"

"Picking huckleberries."

"Why, I believe you're a Yankee," Hadley said.

"No, I ain't . . . but I'm no Secesh."

"How's that; not a Yankee and not a Secesh. What are you?"

"I believe in tendin' to my own business and lettin' other people's alone."

"But would you have the Yankees overrun the South, steal our Negroes, and rob us of our property?"

"Yes, if you don't quit this fightin' and killin'. You all fetched on this war. Fir a few niggers you've driven this country to war, and forced men into the army to fight for you who don't want to go, and you've got the whole country in such a plight that there's nothing goin' on but huntin' and killin', huntin' and killin', all the time."[33]

When Hadley, convinced of the women's loyalty, confessed that he and his companions were Union soldiers, the women gave them shelter and food for several days. Indicative of the complex character of mountain loyalty, however, was the fact that their father was kept ignorant of the arrangement. His landlord was a loyal Confederate and the neighbors were Rebels too. The family feared reprisals if the father were found to be an accomplice to escape efforts. The community was split about half and half by the war, and the brother

33. Hadley, *Seven Months a Prisoner,* 180–81.

of the family had been hiding out in the area as a deserter for eighteen months.

The runaways became local celebrities among the Unionists. They received callers while the father was at work — mostly young women, although an old one-legged man with a bottle of whiskey in his hand also dropped by to pay his respects. The night before they left, the girls even arranged a quiet social evening of candy pulling. Apparently the absence of the young men of the region, who were either in the army or hiding out from the army, pulled the young women in like magnets. Yet there were more serious concerns than courting. Two of the young women set out the first night into the darkness on a six-mile search for guides who would take the bluecoats to Knoxville and safety.[34]

As Confederate forces reached into the mountains to punish Unionists or to conscript them into the army or to capture deserters, the men they sought moved farther into the mountains. They left their homes and lived in the mountains nearby. At night they slept on the hillsides, fearing that the soldiers would sneak up on them as they slept. During the times when the army and the home guards were not near, the mountaineers returned to their homes, planted their crops, hunted, fished, and lived as normally as the conditions allowed. Since the Rebels knew of such habits, however, the outlaws had to be wary of sudden strikes designed to capture them. At home they posted women and children as sentinels to warn them of sudden raids. It was almost a game of hide-and-seek, but it could be a brutal and deadly game.

The Rebels quickly grew tired of this sport, especially when the outlaws took to fighting back and killing their seekers or to staging raids on Rebel forces or homes. Then the brutality began, and it escalated beyond peacetime limits. Victims of mountain violence began to include not just able-bodied men, and the violence was not limited to killing. The soldiers and home guards discovered that while they often could not find the deserters and the Unionists, they could usually find their families and could always find their homes and lands. Often they would burn the cabins and barns, kill all the livestock, destroy or steal anything that might be of use to the out-

34. Ibid. Other escapees received similar treatment — great generosity and treatment as curiosities and/or friends with news. See Drake, *Fast and Loose in Dixie,* 160–63; Richardson, *Secret Service,* 452–53.

laws or their supporters. Sometimes when the soldiers were especially desperate or angry, they would torture those left at home to
force them to tell where the men were. In one instance in the lower
mountains to the east, the Confederates devised a special tactic to
lure deserters and draft dodgers out of the hills. They rounded up
the families of all the men known to be avoiding service and put
them into jail. Women as well as children were taken, and they were
held without food. Then word was sent out that whenever the men
decided to give themselves up, their families would be released.
Most of them came in.[35]

Often the Rebels practiced subterfuge to get the outlaws. Ragged-
looking men would suddenly appear out of the mountains and forests.
They would make their way to a cabin and plead for help in escaping
to Union lines. They would beg shelter and food and ask for guides
to take them to safety. The local Unionists would be suspicious for a
time but then would yield, ask their neighbors to help, and perhaps
call in the men from the hills to act as guides over the mountains.
That night or the next day, Confederate troops would suddenly
show up, the alleged escapees would reveal their true identity, and
the Unionists would be hustled off to jail or to conscript camps.[36]

Out in the mountains, therefore, the men were suspicious, cau-
tious, and usually well armed. Albert Richardson, correspondent
for the *New York Tribune,* met a group of these men during his escape. They were walking arsenals. Each man carried a rifle, one or
two revolvers, a bowie knife, a haversack, and a canteen. Ordinarily
the men were quiet and deliberate, but when the war was mentioned, "their eyes emitted that peculiar glare which I had observed
years before, in Kansas, and which seems inseparable from the
hunted man." They wanted to be left alone, they told Richardson,
but "when the Rebels come to hunt us, we hunt them. They know
that we are in earnest, and that before they can kill any one of us, he
will break a hole in the ice large enough to drag two or three of them
along with him."[37]

35. Burson, *Race for Liberty,* 70–71; Richardson, *Secret Service,* 465–66; Ellis,
Thrilling Adventures, 238–39.
36. Burson, *Race for Liberty,* 118–19; Hadley, *Seven Months a Prisoner,* 228–30;
Drake, *Fast and Loose in Dixie,* 149; Ellis, *Thrilling Adventures,* 210–11.
37. Richardson, *Secret Service,* 465–66; Lieutenant A. Cooper, *In and Out of
Rebel Prisons* (Oswego, N.Y.: Oliphant, 1888), 177–86.

It was easy for escaping prisoners and local Unionists to make heroes of such men. Many of them were romantic bandits — Robin Hoods fighting for their cause, robbing when necessary, but robbing only from those rich Confederates who could afford to "donate" food and other necessities to the poor. Living among the people yet riding out or marching out to danger and possible glory, risking their lives for helpless escapees, enduring cold and wet, exhaustion and death — they were almost perfect heroes. Their risks, their wounds, their deeds were present, known, and experienced by those around them. Unlike soldiers far away, these men were living, touchable idols.

Yet there was another side to the mountain raiders, a side that revealed them as vicious criminals, not brave bandits.[38] Many of them took the opportunity brought by the war to revenge old debts, to loot, plunder, and terrorize in the name of defending themselves and preserving the Union. Others, made desperate by being hunted men, could not afford to discriminate very carefully between those who could afford to be robbed and those who could not, between those who were Rebels from conviction and those who were Rebels by coercion. They seldom had the chance to question a Rebel soldier absent from his home on such matters and rarely were willing to ask the families they plundered. And, of course, it was easy for them to rationalize what they did. Their own families and farms were the frequent victims of Confederate plundering, and no one seemed too eager to make such distinctions in their behalf. Furthermore, the division of wealth and class that often divided Unionist and Rebel gave the outlaws reason to believe that, by definition, Rebels could afford to be victims. And the outlaws' desire to avenge their own sufferings further guaranteed that mountain raiding would be brutal.

Few Rebel homes and farms could feel completely safe from these guerrilla forces, whose definition of Rebel was often broad: anyone who had something worth stealing. By the summer of 1863, a young first lieutenant was reporting from Cherokee County that such men "are a terror to the citizens, especially the soldier's wives who are alone. They are killing cattle, sheep and hogs, also stealing bee-gums, breaking smoke houses, milk houses." They were especially trying

38. See J.S. Hobsbawm, *Bandits* (London: Weidenfeld & Nicolson, 1969), *passim.*

to kill officers who sought to organize Confederate companies.[39]

Justified by mutual cruelty, energized by the desperation both sides felt, nurtured by an environment in which betrayal was a constant possibility, the mountain warfare escalated in savagery. More often than not, it was the Unionists who were the victims. Johnson and Carter counties in Tennessee, on the North Carolina border, serve as an example, possibly the most extreme example, of the character of brutality in the mountain warfare and of the success of anti-Unionist gangs. From November 1863 through the winter of 1864 four guerrilla bands rampaged through these counties, killing almost without discrimination, ravaging Union lands. In November of 1863 a man named Whicher led a group into Carter County that killed nine alleged Unionists before leaving. The next fall saw the entry of one of the bloodiest of the anti-Unionist guerrillas, Bill Parker, into Johnson County. Throughout September and October of 1864, Parker and his men were credited with murdering eleven men, four of them over sixty years of age. He also drove large numbers of women and children from the county, burned homes and barns, and slaughtered livestock. Outrage against Parker grew so strong that a band of Unionists hunted him down and finally killed him late in the fall of 1864. No sooner was Parker stopped than two other Rebel irregular leaders, B.H. Duvall and R.C. Bozen, began depredations in Carter and Johnson counties. Both were noted for killing several alleged Unionists, for destroying property and livestock, and Bozen was charged with killing and torturing the Unionists he captured.[40]

In the midst of bloodshed and reprisal, the Confederate government struggled with the task of bringing peace to the mountains. Perhaps if that could be done, the mass of citizens who wanted simply to be left alone would support the secession cause. The development of a policy, however, defied resolution. Too much blood had been shed; too much hatred generated. Solutions that were offered met counterproposals that urged the opposite. Throughout the summer of 1862 authorities debated a resolution. Major General Samuel Jones proposed leniency and promised citizens in the East

39. *OR*, ser. 4, vol. 2, 732-34; Hadley, *Seven Months a Prisoner*, 211-13.
40. Ellis, *Thrilling Adventures*, 289-305; 321-51.

Tennessee district that his soldiers would stop depredations against civilian property. He urged President Davis to support this move toward deescalation by suspending the conscription act so that those fleeing the draft might at least return home to harvest their crops.

Secretary of War G.W. Randolph opposed the policy. Leniency, he insisted, had done nothing to benefit the cause. He pushed Davis for a vigorous enforcement of conscription. Davis asked the governor of Tennessee for his opinion and then supported Randolph — which meant that the status quo endured. Unionists and Rebels clawed and gouged each other in vicious partisan warfare. Detachments of Confederate soldiers drew duty chasing armed "Tories" and "bushwhackers" who found shelter within the mountains among friends. And the loyalty of mountaineers to the Union endured.[41]

Union raids uncovered such loyalty in unexpected places — for example, in gray uniforms. In December 1862 Samuel Carter, now elevated to the rank of general, returned to the mountains with about 2,000 Federal soldiers to raid the region near the town of Union, Tennessee. A detachment of men under Colonel J.P.T. Carter was sent to take the town and to destroy the railroad bridge over the Holston River. Defending the place were two companies of the Rebel Sixty-second North Carolina regiment, but it was a strange sort of defense. When Carter and his men attacked, the Rebels surrendered almost immediately. About 150 men were taken prisoner and paroled on their honor not to take up arms again against the Union. They did so gladly. By the afternoon of the "battle," these warriors were "on their way to the mountains of North Carolina," swearing they would never be exchanged. Their "joy at being captured," Carter reported, "seemed to be unbounded." Furthermore, this raid by Carter seemed to unleash a wave of plundering and robbery by Unionists in the region, action that involved men and boys from Shelton Laurel. North Carolina troops in regular service were withdrawn from that duty and sent back to protect loyal Confederates in the region.[42]

Although Unionism endured in the mountains, it did not flourish, for the Unionists had enemies more ominous than soldiers. Gunfire, battles, and skirmishes were the most blatant announce-

41. *OR* ser. 1, vol. 16, pt. 2, 893–95, 952–58.
42. Humes, *Loyal Mountaineers,* App.; Cotton, "Appalachian North Carolina," 137.

ments that the war was invading the mountains, but more insidious signs appeared too. By the winter of 1862 the mountain people began to suffer from the deprivations of the necessities of everyday life. These hardships were perhaps more difficult to tolerate and comprehend than the sudden and bloody intrusions that were unique to war. They were signs that life could not roll on unchanged while battle raged elsewhere. The sudden killings and brutalities of war could be understood as incidents of war—expected occurrences, however tragic to the families involved. Violent death, heartwrenching though it may be, was the unusual occurrence and daily life went on. There was food to grow, clothing to make, children to rear—this stream of life went on—this abided. War brought violent killing, but it could not touch this. There is a haiku that says, "Sipping a cup of tea, I stopped the war." But what if there were no tea; what if the war should produce not just unusual violence—what if it should attack the abiding rhythm of everyday life?

By the fall and winter of 1862, this is exactly what happened. Nature provided conditions that, linked to the deprivations of war, produced grim want in the mountains of western North Carolina. Enlistments and conscription took away the farmers of the region and kept them away from planting and harvest. Confederate raids forced deserters and guerrilla bands to stay on the run. They could not regularly use their plows and scythes. And the mutual killing, the burning of barns, houses, and fields, the slaughter of livestock all crippled the productivity of the region's farms.[43]

By the fall of 1862 cotton, clothing, wool, corn, and hogs—all vital to the lives of mountaineers—were almost impossible to get. Speculators hung on to their supplies of grain, refusing to sell for the Confederate money they were offered or insisting that people pay them in bank notes—not a widely held currency in poor mountain regions. Furthermore, distillers were willing to pay twice as much for the grain as food suppliers or the general public. Those who could not pay these prices had no bread, and often they were the families of soldiers away from home. By December 1862 the congressmen and senators from the mountain districts were pleading with President Davis to suspend conscription in their region so

43. Samuel A. Ashe, *History of North Carolina,* vol. 2 (Raleigh, N.C.: Edwards, and Broughton), 660–61.

that men could come out of hiding and be able to help their families. In November 1862 the *Raleigh Register* spoke of the "fearful suffering" of the winter that would affect not only the impoverished but even those who thought themselves comfortable. It issued a warning to food speculators that "speculation in human life is not the safest business [considering] both person and purse, for men to engage in." By early March the *Raleigh Weekly Standard* looked at the western part of the state and wondered "How Are Soldiers' Wives to Get Bread?"[44]

The most eloquent testimony came from the sufferers themselves, not their spokesmen. One mountain citizen wrote to a Raleigh editor, "Will you be so kind, Mr. Editor, as to inform Jeff Davis and his Destructives, that after they take the next draw of men from this mountain region, if they please, as an act of *great* and *special* mercy be so gracious as to call out a *few*, just a few of their exempted pets . . . to knock the women and children of the mountains in the head, to put them out of their misery." And there was misery. When a young private named Edward Cooper was put on trial for his life for desertion, he offered in defense the following letter from his wife: "My Dear Edward—I have always been proud of you, and since your connection with the Confederate army I have been prouder than ever before. I would not have you do anything wrong for the world, but before God, Edward, unless you come home, we must die. Last night I was aroused by little Eddie's crying. I called, 'What's the matter, Eddie?' and he said, 'Oh, Mama, I'm so hungry.' And Lucy, Edward, your darling Lucy, she never complains, but she is growing thinner and Edward, unless you come home we must die."[45]

No deprivation hit harder than that of salt. Imaginative people might invent substitutes for most of the things they ate, but there was no substitute for salt. Before the advent of refrigeration, the only means of preserving meat were smoking and salt, and at slaughtering time, between December and February, the need for

44. *Raleigh Weekly Register,* Nov. 15, 1862; *North Carolina Weekly Standard,* March 11, 1863; Cotton, "Appalachian North Carolina," 99–101.
45. Quoted in Barrett, *Civil War in North Carolina,* 191, from D.H. Hill, "The Women of the Confederacy," in *Addresses at the Unveiling of the Memorial to the North Carolina Women of the Confederacy* (Raleigh, N.C.: Edwards, and Broughton, 1914). Also quoted in Lonn, *Desertion During the Civil War,* 12–13.

salt was especially desperate. Without it the meager supply of meat that the poor had would simply rot within a few weeks' time. They would be left without a staple of their diet. As Governor John Shorter of Alabama wrote, "There is scarcely any misfortune which can befall us which will produce such widespread complaint and dissatisfaction." He believed that Alabamans at home might be able to shift for themselves if their men were around to help, but "the families of our soldiers, far away, helpless and poor, appeal to us in language that cannot fail to excite our profoundest sympathies."[46]

North Carolina was especially hard hit by the salt famine. The state, having no internal sources, imported most of its salt from the mines at Saltville, Virginia. This supply, however, was imperiled by its closeness to Union forces and was being drained by demands from other Rebel states no longer able to rely on northern sources. To counteract threats to the Tarheel supply, Governor Vance in December 1861 established an office of salt commissioner to encourage and coordinate the manufacture and sale of salt.

Salt works were set up on the coast to draw salt from the sea. This strategy, however, was undercut by the threat of Union invasions, by disease among the workers, by the impressment of salt workers into the army, and by conflicts between the state and the Richmond government over control of the salt works. The brutal winter of 1862–63, which made it almost impossible to move the commodity from Saltville into North Carolina, further diminished supplies. Skyrocketing prices pointed up the need for salt. Raleigh reported prices rising from $12 to $100 for a two-bushel sack. By that winter the cry for salt was reaching a crescendo. Threats of raids by private citizens against the salt works in Virginia suggested the desperation. A correspondent from Ashe County wrote Vance that salt was urgently needed there or the supply of hogs would be lost. There were thousands of bushels of salt in Saltville, he claimed, and "we the citizens of Ashe has come to the conclusion to go and take it by force if the owners of it won't let us have it for a fare price. . . . we wish your advice . . . whether we can be seriously punished or not. . . . we are compelled to have salt while it can be had or we will fight for it." Other mountain counties had equally serious shortages. The sit-

46. Ella Lonn, *Salt as a Factor in the Confederacy* (New York: W. Neale, 1933), 16–17, 41–42.

uation in Yancy County was so desperate that no one could be found to take the position of salt agent. By the late fall of 1862, Vance had issued a proclamation placing an embargo on the export of salt from the state. He also was encouraging trade between loyal Confederates and Unionists so that his state could get salt in trade for its turpentine and cotton.[47]

This statewide want translated into cruel deprivation in the mountains. As in all cases of need, the poor felt it most brutally. Half-intelligible appeals poured into the governor's office. The pathetic calls reminded historian Ella Lonn of "a child's cries to its parents for help." Governor Vance responded with compassion to relieve the suffering, but in Madison County, Confederates took the lack of this necessity in the Union regions as an opportunity to punish their enemies. Whatever meager amounts of salt that did arrive in the county seat of Marshall were hoarded by the loyal Rebels and kept from the hands of poor rural mountaineers suspected of Union sympathies. The tactic seems to have been designed not only to punish but also to drive the deserters from their hideouts into the towns. Unfortunately for the Confederates, the tactic worked.

---

47. Ibid., 82–83, 89–107; *Raleigh Weekly Register,* Nov. 15, 1862; Salisbury *Carolina Watchman,* Jan. 12, 1863; Muriel Sheppard, *Cabins in the Laurels* (Chapel Hill: Univ. of North Carolina Press, 1935) 61–62.

4

THE KILLING

Wherever the vandal cometh,
Press home to his heart your steel,
And when at his bosom you can not,
Like the serpent, go strike at his
heel.

Through thicket and wood go hunt
him,
Creep up to his camp-fire side,
And let ten of his corpses blacken
Where one of our brothers hath
died.

In his fainting, foot-sore marches,
In his flight from the stricken fray,
In the snare of the lonely ambush,
The debts we own him pay.

S. TEACKLE WALLIS,
"The Guerrillas" (1864)

Although it was the county seat, Marshall hardly looked the part. The French Broad River rushed by its doorsteps. From behind, a steep mountain seemed to be trying to push the town into the river. There was hardly room for the town to stand, let alone grow. Residents had managed to squeeze in nine houses, three stores, a shoemaker shop, a blacksmith, and two hotels. The better of the two stood a story and a half tall and contained four bedrooms. The only indications of the town's official importance were a dilapidated brick courthouse and a decayed wooden jail.[1]

Nevertheless, late one evening in early January 1863, a band of about fifty men were very interested in Marshall. Many were deserters from the Sixty-fourth North Carolina, a regiment drawn from the surrounding countryside. All were mountain people—uneducated, poor, considered almost uncivilized by those from more comfort-

1. *New York Tribune*, Aug. 10, 1871.

able places—and several were from Shelton Laurel. The raiders were cold, suffering from want, and especially desperate for salt. And they had little affection for Colonel Lawrence M. Allen, commander of the Sixty-fourth, or for any other Rebel sympathizers, for that matter. They were ready to satisfy both their needs and their hatreds in the sleeping town.

Home on leave, Mrs. Allen's kinsman Captain John Peek of the Sixty-fourth was awakened by noises and went to investigate. The raiders shot him, shattering his right arm, and began plundering the stores of salt. Other items that struck their attention also were taken, especially clothing and blankets, for the winter was bitterly cold. The men moved quickly to Colonel Allen's house. Some of his servants were at home, as were Mrs. Allen and her three children—two of them deathly ill with scarlet fever. The raiders broke into the house and began taking whatever they valued. Then they demanded that Mrs. Allen give them the keys to the trunks and bureaus. When she refused, they took an axe and broke the locks open and took what they wanted: clothes, money, and shoes. A friend of Allen's later claimed that they even stole the children's clothing from beside their beds. As the raiders left town, they plundered a few of the houses on the outskirts and then dispersed and melted back into the mountains.[2]

Ironically, at the very time that Unionists were raiding Marshall, the Sixty-fourth was in Bristol, Tennessee, near Saltville, Virginia, guarding salt supplies there. Hearing of this raid, the leaders of the unit, Allen and James Keith, asked commanding officer Henry Heth to let them punish the guilty parties. Allen's status at the time is unclear. He had been suspended without pay for six months from January to July 1862 for reporting a soldier present who, in fact, was in Richmond on personal business. Presumably, by the end of July that suspension had expired. When the newspapers reported on the massacre, however, they said that he was again on suspension, this time for "crime and drunkenness." In any event, he was with his troops at the time of the killings, although he did not command them. Command was in the hands of Keith, directing the unit that Allen had recruited and trained. It would be Keith's orders that would make the soldiers fire.[3]

2. *OR*, ser. 1, vol. 18, 810–11, 853–54, 867; Gaston, *Partisan Campaigns*, 10–11.
3. *New York Times*, July 24, 1863; *Memphis Bulletin*, July 15, 1863; Orders and

Heth approached the meeting with Keith at a moment in his life likely to spawn at least misunderstanding. He had been rebuked in his effort for promotion. He had been summarily transferred into the East Tennessee command. He had lost a chance to gain a victory in the Kentucky campaign. His experiences with mountain warfare in both West Virginia and East Tennessee could only have embittered him. And he was looking forward to the day when his transfer would come and he could join his friend and protector Robert E. Lee, leaving behind the frustrations and reminders of a staggering career.

Yet his physical appearance when Keith met him probably belied these difficulties. He was a handsome man with dark hair and eyes and a full moustache that reached almost to his chin. He retained the aristocratic bearing of a Virginia nobleman, yet he was not aloof. Heth charmed those he met with warmth and an infectious sense of humor that he could turn on himself as well as on others. Despite being only thirty-seven, he carried with him almost fifteen years of command, and the stars of a Confederate general could not be ignored.

The man Heth saw must have radiated danger. Thirty-five-year-old James Keith was tall and lean and had a slim face, a high forehead, and prominent cheekbones. His black hair and beard and his dark complexion sharply contrasted his gray-blue eyes. To Heth, who epitomized the culture and traditions of the Old Dominion, Keith must have seemed a part of the wild, almost uncivilized, southern highlands. Here was no misbegotten cadet. Here was a dangerous man, a leader of what the army called partisan rangers, of men who made their own rules of warfare, if they could be called rules.[4]

Keith's accomplishments, if Heth knew of them, were easily ignored or explained; distinction in the mountains might arise from abilities scorned in Virginia society. Even if he understood Keith's status in Madision County, Heth knew it might be very useful in such an assignment.

Circulars, General Orders no. 35, Dept. of East Tennessee, Record Group 109, National Archives, Washington, D.C.; Gaston, *Partisan Campaigns,* 11.

4. Keith described in "A Proclamation," announcing his escape from jail, *North Carolina Standard,* March 10, 1869. Heth description based on Douglas Freeman, *Lee's Lieutenants,* vol. 2 (New York: Scribners, 1946) 506–507, and portrait in Morrison, ed., *Memoirs of Henry Heth* facing 151.

As the two men faced each other, the citizen soldier met the professional; the mountain leader, a stranger to the rules of military behavior, met his commanding officer, a man with years of service and experience. Keith was dependent on Heth not only for orders but for explanations of their meanings should circumstances render their meanings obscure. The general surely knew the rules and certainly understood the effects that guerrilla warfare had on orders and rules.

Although Heth knew the proper standards of conduct, he had many reasons for believing that Keith did not. In addition to being an untrained soldier, the colonel was also a man personally involved in what happened at Marshall. And he was a man with first-hand experience in guerrilla fighting, a man with scores to settle. Not only was it likely that Keith did not know the rules, but he had powerful reasons for not wanting to know. As a result, Heth's orders took on major importance.

The general's responsibility for making things very clear was inescapable, for the ambiguous situation in the mountains cried out for careful handling. And the main area where such care was required was in the proper way to deal with irregular "soldiers," the type of men responsible for the Marshall raid.

International law distinguished the treatment of guerrilla fighters from that afforded regular troops. Regular soldiers fought in uniform, attacked military targets according to the orders of superiors, and generally engaged in fighting that exposed both sides to the same risks of being killed, captured, or wounded. Regular soldiers earned the right to be treated as prisoners of war. If captured, they were not to be punished as individuals for killing or destroying. They were to be protected and treated with respect.

Guerrillas, on the other hand, attacked and fled, disguised themselves as civilians, shot noncombatants, rampaged without orders from responsible superiors. They refused to take the same risks as soldiers. Their tactics, of course, were forced on them by their location within enemy lines and their immensely less powerful military status. International law, however, took the viewpoint of regular armies and treated irregulars as criminals, not soldiers. If engaged by regulars, guerrillas could be shot even if they threw down their arms and begged to surrender. They had no right to be treated as prisoners of war.

A subtle distinction emerged at this point, a distinction easily forgotten by poorly trained citizen soldiers but understood by a career professional like Heth. While guerrillas could be killed if engaged in battle and could be denied the right to become prisoners, once they had been captured they could not be executed without legal proceedings to determine their status as guerrillas and their guilt for killing or destroying. A military or a civilian court had to try them. Execution of a prisoner without such a proceeding was murder.[5]

Keith later insisted that the general told him, "I want no reports from you about your course at Laurel. I do not want to be troubled with any prisoners and the last one of them should be killed." The colonel further said that Heth complained about getting too many prisoners from the Laurel region. He did not want any more of them sent to Knoxville. Two witnesses supported this description of Heth's orders.

Faced with these accusations, Heth admitted saying to Keith that "those found in arms ought not to be treated as enemies [that is, as regular soldiers], and in the event of an engagement with them to take no prisoners as [I] considered that they had forfeited all such claims." The general insisted, however, that he had not "use[d] . . . any remarks which would authorize maltreatment of prisoners who had been accepted as such or to women or children."[6]

Heth had not used remarks that would authorize maltreatment of prisoners or of women and children, that was true. He had let silence speak. He had not explained the crucial intricacies of the law of partisan warfare, at least the law that outsiders applied. Yet Heath knew the true rules of that game. He had been in Mexico, on the western plains, in the mountains of western Virginia. And perhaps also he did not know, in that special way that commanders have of not knowing such things, a way that permits but does not demand, a way that lets them wash their hands and maybe even believe that their hands are clean. Heth denied the crime of giving an order. He did not deny the sin of remaining silent. He may not have felt sinful.[7]

5. Henry Wheaton, *Elements of International Law* (Philadelphia: Lea and Blanchard, 1846), 406; Francis Lieber, "Guerrilla Parties," in *Miscellaneous Writings of Francis Lieber,* vol. 2 (Philadelphia: Lippincott, 1881), 277–92 (first published in 1862); *Opinions of the Attorney General of the United States* (Washington, D.C., 1865), 307–308.
6. James A. Seddon to Zebulon Vance, May 23, 1863, *OR,* ser. 2, vol. 5, 956.
7. On indirect permission to commit evil, see Nevitt Sanford, Craig Comstock

The Marshall raid had shaken the army and civilian authorities. They were not sure who the raiders were and what the raid meant — was it the beginning of an uprising led by Unionist forces? Confederates prepared a response for these "traitors," "Tories," and "bushwhackers," especially for those of Shelton Laurel.

A force under General W.G.M. Davis was already in the field trying to find out what had happened in Madison County. The Sixty-fourth was ordered to join them. Rumors began after the raid that an organized unit of up to five hundred men were beginning operations in the region, that towns, barns, and bridges, the property of all Confederate sympathizers, were targeted for destruction. Their next assignment would be to attack travelers on the road to Asheville and to destroy the stage line operating in the region. Governor Zeb Vance alerted local militia units in the area, and they began scouring the county and neighboring counties for the raiders and their supporters.[8]

General Davis ordered Captain Nelson's company to move into the Laurel Valley to investigate and to engage the enemy if found. Nelson's force did find some of the "Tories," killed twelve of them, and captured twenty. All but one or two of those killed were said to have been deserters from Allen's regiment. Davis also ordered Major W.N. Garrett to take 200 men, a company of cavalry, and about 30 Indians and "pursue and arrest every man in the mountains, of known bad character, whether engaged in any of the late outrages or not." This force was to be part of a larger operation throughout the mountain region that would involve six companies of cavalry, Colonel W.H. Thomas's legion of whites, and 200 Indians, and would cover the mountains of Tennessee and Georgia as well as North Carolina. Meanwhile Davis's superior, General Heth, wrote to Governor Vance to assure him that every effort would be made to bring peace and order to the mountains of his state. Vance was a mountaineer himself and knew the people well. He was worried about summary "justice" in an environment that produced many pressures on men's loyalties. He wrote Heth to express his hope that "you will

---

and Associates, *Sanctions for Evil* (San Francisco: Jossey-Bass, 1971), 6, 21, 94–95, 193.

8. J.W. Woodfin to Governor Vance, Feb. 1, 1863; *OR,* ser. 1, vol. 18, 810–11, 853–54, 867.

not relax until the tories are crushed," but sought to interpose a shield against unnecessary brutality. "Do not let our excited people deal too harshly with these misguided men," he added. "Please have the captured delivered to the proper authorities for trial." As Vance wrote these words, units of the Sixty-fourth were returning home to punish the "Tories," deserters, and "bushwhackers." Two columns were moving into the Laurel valley, one from its mouth, the other from its crest. Allen led the first, Keith the second.[9]

Up to this point the war had not brought Allen success equal to his civilian efforts, and probably not equal to his hopes. Yet he had had opportunities to use his influence in profitable ways. Although smarting from having his unit demoted from cavalry to infantry and from his suspension, Allen was benefitting from his power as commander, if not militarily, at least personally. He was engaged in the practice of forceably conscripting men into the army and then extorting money from them for their release.[10] Obviously he was not above doing whatever he thought would advance his career. He certainly felt even fewer compunctions about avenging a personal grievance. He was "not an attractive man," one officer observed, "rather otherwise." He was however, "fearless and brave." It was a frightening combination for anyone who obstructed or, worse, threatened him.[11]

James Keith might not have been able to impress General Heth, but to the men he led toward Shelton Laurel he was a man to respect and maybe even fear. Wealthy, ambitious, intelligent, he was remembered later as a "soldier," a "fighter," "fearless" and capable of cruelty should the war make cruelty necessary.[12]

There is some possibility that the two men were related by blood.

9. W.G.M. Davis to Vance, Jan. 21, 1868, Heth to Vance, Jan. 21, 1863, Vance to Heth, Jan. 21, 1863, *OR*, ser. 1, vol. 18, 810–11, 853–54.

10. Zebulon Vance to James Seddon, Aug. 13, 1863, Record Group 109, Military Service Record of L.M. Allen, National Archives, Washington, D.C.; Vance to Seddon, May 13, 1863, Governors Letterbooks, North Carolina State Archives, Raleigh, N.C.; Allen to Vance, undated, Box 184, Governors Papers, North Carolina Archives. There is a possibility that Keith was involved in this enterprise with Allen. See A.J. Morey to William Garrett, June 1863, Vance Papers, Box 166, North Carolina State Archives, Raleigh, N.C.

11. B.T. Morris, "The Sixty-fourth Regiment," in Walter Clark, ed., *Histories of the Several Regiments and Battalions from North Carolina in the Great War, 1861–65*, vol. 5 (Goldsboro, N.C.: Nash Bros. 1901), 661.

12. Ibid.

Keith's middle name was Allen; a young boy named Guthridge Keith lived with Allen's father; and after the war both of these officers, their careers in shambles, would escape to Arkansas.[13] Whether or not they were kin, they were related by class, by drive and ambition, and by the fact that they had a score to settle in Shelton Laurel. For Allen there was the vicious ransacking of his home, the terrorizing of his wife and children, and the wounding of his kinsman, John Peek. For Keith there was the death of his nephew Mitchell Keith, who had left his uncle's home to enlist in the Sixty-fourth and was dead at age fourteen, killed shortly after Keith organized his company in May 1862. The two men, already the elected leaders of their units, now had even more compelling reasons to assert that leadership to gain revenge.

The members of the Sixty-fourth Regiment, as they marched into the mountains, could look back on a short, frustrating, inglorious history. Although some of the troops had served for over a year and a half, most were men who had joined the unit the previous summer. And many of them were not soldiers by choice. A sweep of the mountains had resulted in many enlistments under threat of a fate worse than military service. It was at this time that several of the Sheltons had been swept up into the army, but as soon as they had the chance, they deserted and returned home. Others, no doubt, envied them and waited for their chance to desert. Devotion to the regiment and the Confederacy was not deep seated. In August 1862 the Sixty-fourth Regiment was described as "new and [hardly] organized." Even after a year of service, when in June almost the entire regiment was captured at Cumberland Gap, the commander recalled it as "small, having been reduced by desertions, at one time three hundred in a body."[14]

The officers of the regiment, however, remained loyal and were bound together by class and kinship as well as duty. Allen's relatives, Alfred, Levi, and John Peek, and Keith's kin, William and Thomas Keith, led an officer corps woven with similar relation-

13. Manuscript Census, 1860, Madison County, N.C.; Military Service Records, 64th North Carolina Regiment, Record Group 109, National Archives, Washington, D.C.

14. *OR*, ser. 1, vol. 16, 2, 773–74; vol. 30, pt. 2, 611; Military Service Records, 64th North Carolina Regiment, Record Group 109, microfilm reels 556, 558, National Archives, Washington, D.C.; Morris, "Sixth-fourth Regiment," 659–60.

ships. And those for whom records survive were well off.[15]

To these leaders and the loyal soldiers they commanded, the deserters must have been especially loathsome. Not only did desertion increase the physical danger to those who stayed, but it created a burning sense of betrayal mixed with envy. After all, the deserters had done what the loyal soldiers often must have longed to do—run away from the threat of death, the dysentery, the lousy food and literally lousy clothes, the sleeping in snow and rain, the experience of constantly being either bored to the edge of pain or terrified into numbness. Deserters slept at home, with their wives, played with their children, and came and went as they chose so long as Confederate troops were not near.

The Sixty-fourth seemed bogged down in vicious, absurd duty, "moved about 'from pillar to post,'" as one officer recalled, on "tramps, marches, and scouts [where] very few comforts were furnished." Its first assignment had been to act as guards in Knoxville, where they trained. Then they were sent to scout the mountainsides trying to find, fight, or capture Unionists. Their success was minimal, the sort that such duty usually brings: a few captured deserters, a few enemy shot, but never a chance to gain anything resembling a victory or even a fight. One of the leaders later recalled, "They never gave us a fair fight, square up, face to face, man to man, horse to horse." And as the environment of guerrilla warfare built frustration, it also urged that men lose control of themselves. In the West Virginia mountains a Union soldier hunting southern partisans wrote to his parents of capturing a "moccasin ranger" who had "run in the woods till he did not know whether he was a wild beast or a human being! Some times I think we are almost out of the world. . . . And I expect if we stay here much longer we will all get wild!"[16]

So, on that January day, the Sixty-fourth once again moved into the mountains to chase down guerrilla snipers. The usual terrors could be anticipated: gunfire from an unknown spot, perhaps a comrade suddenly falling dead, and the frustrating anger at and

---

15. Manuscript Census, 1860, Madison County, N.C.; John W. Moore, *Roster of North Carolina Troops in the War Between the States*, vol. 4, 51–81.

16. Morris, "Sixty-fourth Regiment," 661, 664; *OR*, ser. 1, vol. 16, pt. 2, 893; Union soldier quoted in Richard O. Curry, *A House Divided: A Study of Statehood Politics in West Virginia* (Pittsburgh: Univ. of Pittsburgh Press, 1964), 76.

loathing of an enemy that could not be seen and, worse, could not be fought, captured, or killed. This time, if anything, it was worse. Heavy snow fell throughout the march. It was cruelly cold, and marching became almost impossible at times. Keith's column descending from the high regions at the top of the creek was especially hindered; almost twenty-five of his men were frostbitten. As the two groups approached the settled portion of the valley, they could hear the signal horns of the foe sounding. Then as they moved deeper into the valley, gunfire began from behind rocks and trees, snowbanks, and laurel thickets. At first Allen's men met only scattered resistance, but they managed to kill eight of the enemy. Then at Bill Shelton's place they encountered, at last, a force of about fifty who, after a sharp skirmish and a charge by cavalry, were driven off leaving six dead. Allen camped at Bill Shelton's and waited for Keith to arrive. Later that evening Keith and his men apparently straggled in.[17]

Sometime during that night Colonel Allen was awakened suddenly. There was a message for him from Marshall. His son, Romulus, age six, had died of scarlet fever. His daughter, Margaret, age four, was also stricken and not expected to live. At daylight Allen and four men rode out of camp and raced for Marshall as fast as they could in the heavy snow. They received fire from the surrounding mountains but rode on, despite the fact that Allen's horse received a shot through the withers. At about 10 A.M. he rode into the town and rushed to his house. There he found the dead body of his son and his dying daughter. Soon she, too, was dead.

In the morning a grieving Lawrence Allen and his wife buried their children. On the next day Allen rejoined his soldiers camped at Shelton Laurel. The men must have heard the story of the death of his children. Although Allen was not a popular man with his troops, his loss must have recharged their hatred for the enemy around them. First was the raid on their county seat and the stories connected with it of the brutality to Allen's sick children. Then there was the march through the snow and freezing cold and the gunshots, sudden and terrible, from the surrounding hills. Now the

17. Gaston, *Partisan Campaigns,* 11; Daniel Ellis, *Thrilling Adventures of Daniel Ellis* (New York: Harper, 1867), 245, 408.

deaths of the children—who could doubt that the savage plundering of Allen's house had been responsible? Something had to be done.

Years later one of Allen's neighbors during the war, a Reverend George H. Bell, would still speak of the justice of the revenge on the bushwhackers. "They soon found out," he said, "that it would have been better to have aroused a lion in his den than to have disturbed Col. Allen's private family circle." Captain B.T. Morris, Company A of the Sixty-fourth, would explain later, "When an officer finds himself and men bushwhacked from behind every shrub, tree, or projection on all sides of the road, only severe measures will stop it."[18]

With Keith commanding, the Sixty-fourth fanned out into the valley, arresting those they deemed dangerous. Hearing of the sweep of the region and fearing capture in the open, three men came into Marshall and turned themselves over to authorities there. Meanwhile the soldiers were at work arresting suspects. A few were turned over to Keith's acting adjutant general—W.H. Bailey. Bailey sent them to General Davis, who was at Warm Springs, but Davis sent them back, saying he wished them to be turned over to the civil authorities for punishment. Bailey arrested four of them and sent them to the Asheville jail. Meanwhile the adjutant had discovered that one of those arrested was a conscript avoiding service and so sent him to the conscript officer in Greeneville. Three others were mere boys, and Bailey asked local prominent citizens what should be done with them. It was agreed that they might be paroled on the condition that they stay and work in Marshall bringing wood and water to the town jail. These men, the ones who made it into Bailey's hands, were the lucky ones.[19]

Out in the surrounding mountains the roundup continued and the prisoners taken there had something else in store for them and for their families. The mood of the soldiers was brutal, for they were in an environment guaranteed to terrorize both soldier and victim and to obscure the distinction between them. Surrounded by hostile people, moving in terrain known intimately by the invisible enemy, it was easy to surrender to brutality. In guerrilla warfare men can feel

18. Gaston, *Partisan Campaigns,* 11-12, 26-27; Morris, "Sixty-fourth Regiment," 661.

19. W.H. Bailey to Vance, Feb. 18, 1863, Governors Papers, State Archives, Raleigh, N.C.

that the environment itself is hostile to them, that each tree or hill-side is dangerous, and that death stalks them. In regular battle death terrorizes, but not to the same extent. There are things in regular combat that a man can do to restrain his fears, to fight back. He can do his job, the job he was trained for. His mind grasps its duties and does them. The necessities of fighting itself demand attention. Fire, return fire, try to spot the enemy, load, reload, charge, get to that tree, that stone wall, that ditch, cover the platoon, kill the bastards. Stand up like a man — face death — dish it out. Do not think, react. The man who hesitates is dead. He can be a warrior, fighting for the cause, risking death, perhaps provoking it a little, doing something to work off the guilt that comes from not being dead when good friends are.

There was no such duty for the Sixty-fourth. Instead there was only a hidden enemy, a death, a maiming — that could not be stalked but that stalked each man. It chose the time. It chose the place. Each man was a victim and could only brood about it, not act. There was no heroism, no warriorlike glory, no way to meet the fear. There was only the fear. And even if a man got lucky and found the enemy, what was he? Sometimes an armed man or two, but sometimes just a kid with a rifle.

And there were the things you had to do to find the sneaking bushwhackers, to get back at them, to stop them from killing you, from making you hurt. You had to hunt the mountaineers down, go to their cabins, frightened every step by what might come flying from a laurel grove. And then the hunted men were not there, only the women, but the women knew. They had to know where the men were, but they would not tell you, so you had to make them tell you — threaten them, whip them, then if they still kept quiet, tie a rope around their necks, toss it over a tree branch, and raise them into the air until they began to strangle, faces turning blue. Then you let them down and asked them again, "Where are the men?"

They claimed they did not know, but they had to know. They had to know to justify what you were doing to them. Some talked, some did not. Almost no one died from what you did, but you had made them pay. Then as you left, you killed the livestock so that they enemy would not have provision and maybe you burned the barn or the house itself. Then you ride or walk away and hate them all the more for what they were making you do, for what they were making you be, for making you find that sometimes you liked it — Jesus, God — sometimes you liked it.[20]

As the hunt in Shelton Laurel went on, it was the fortunate women and old people who had their men taken from them. Those unfortunate enough to be relatives of suspects that the troops could not find were whipped and tortured and hanged until almost dead and then let down again for more questioning. Eighty-five-year-old Mrs. Unus Riddle was whipped, hanged temporarily, and robbed. Seventy-year-old Sally Moore was whipped with hickory rods until the blood ran down her back. Another woman, the mother of an infant child, was tied in the snow to a tree and her baby placed in the doorway of her cabin. Unless she talked, the soldiers told her, they would leave them both there. Sarah and Mary Shelton, wives of two suspected Marshall raiders, were whipped and suspended by ropes around their necks. A young mentally retarded girl named Martha White was beaten and tied by the neck all day to a tree.[21]

Finally Keith's soldiers had taken fifteen men prisoner. Most were captured quietly at home or in the valley. A few tried to run and hide when they saw the troops coming but did not make it. Perhaps five of those captured had taken part in the Marshall raid. The other eight were not involved in that action, whatever their other crimes might have been.[22]

20. For the reactions of soldiers to guerrilla combat, I have drawn on Robert J. Lifton, *Home from the War: Vietnam Veterans Neither Victims nor Executioners* (New York: Simon and Schuster, 1973), 42–56; Joseph Goldstein, Burke Marshall, and Jack Schwartz, eds., *The My Lai Massacre and its Coverup: Beyond the Reach of Law? The Peers Commission Report with a Supplement and Introductory Essay on the Limits of Law* (New York: Free Press, 1976); William Barry Gault, "Some Remarks on Slaughter," *American Journal of Psychiatry* 128 (Oct. 1971), 450–54; Chiam Shatan, "The Grief of Soldiers," *American Journal of Orthopsychiatry* 43 (July 1973), 640–54; Joel Yager, "Personal Violence in Infantry Combat," *Archives of General Psychiatry* 32 (Feb. 1975), 257–61; Philip Caputo, *A Rumor of War* (New York: Holt, 1977); Charles Anderson, *The Grunts* (San Rafael, Calif.: Presidio Press, 1976). For reactions to regular combat I have found most helpful Norman Mailer, *The Naked and the Dead* (New York: Holt, 1951); Samuel Stouffer et al., *The American Soldier* (Princeton, N.J.: Princeton Univ. Press, 1949); Peter Bourne, *Men, Stress, and Vietnam* (Boston: Little, Brown, 1970), 113–14; J. Glenn Gray, *The Warriors: Reflections on Men in Battle* (New York, Harper, 1959); John Keegan, *The Face of Battle* (New York: Viking, 1975).

21. *New York Times,* July 24, 1863, 3; *North Carolina Standard,* April 22, 1863; Ellis, *Thrilling Adventures,* 413–16.

22. A.S. Merrimon to Governor Vance, Feb. 16, 1863, Feb. 24, 1863, in *OR,*

Keith told the prisoners that they would be taken to Tennessee, probably Knoxville, to face a trial by military commission for their alleged misdeeds. Although the prisoners probably did not know it, this announcement was an ominous one, for General Davis had sent prisoners thought to be involved in the Marshall raid to Asheville, to be dealt with by civilian justice. The officers of the Sixty-fourth had other plans for their prisoners. For some reason the fifteen were kept in the Laurel valley over the weekend. Perhaps there was an argument over their fate. Perhaps Keith was hoping to round up more. Early in a morning late in January 1863 Keith's men roused the prisoners out of bed. Two had escaped during the night, but the rest were told to prepare to march. They were moving toward Knoxville.

The file of soldiers and prisoners proceeded on the road to Knoxville for a few miles. Then suddenly the prisoners were stopped. The place was open — near the creek where observers could see what happened to "bushwhackers" and "Tories." There was no warning, no explanation. Five of them were ordered to kneel down. Ten paces away a file of soldiers stood, their guns ready. Then the prisoners knew what was going to happen. Sixty-year-old Joe Woods cried out, "For God's sake, men, you are not going to shoot us? If you are going to murder us at least give us time to pray." Someone begged Keith to remember his promise of a trial. He ignored both statements. He ordered his soldiers to fire. The prisoners put their hands over their faces and begged for mercy. The soldiers hesitated. Despite what they had suffered, some refused to obey the command. "Fire or you will take their place," Keith told them. The soldiers raised their guns, the victims shuddered, the word to fire was given, and four of the men died instantly. A fifth had only been wounded. Writhing in agony from a wound in the stomach, he begged for mercy. One of the soldiers finished the job by shooting the prisoner in the head.

Five more prisoners were ordered to kneel down. Among this group was David Shelton, age thirteen. He pleaded with the soldiers not to kill him. "You have killed my father and brothers," he said. "You have shot my father in the face; do not shoot me in the face." The soldiers fired. Five victims fell, but again one remained. It was

---

ser. 1, vol. 18, 881, 893; *New York Times*, July 24, 1863; *Memphis Bulletin*, July 15, 1863.

David Shelton. He moved to an officer, pleading, "You have killed my old father and my three brothers; you have shot me in both arms — I forgive you all this — I can get well. Let me go home to my mother and sisters." They dragged him back to the execution spot and shot him dead. The remaining three men took their turn and died.[23]

The killing finished, the soldiers dug a shallow mass grave and dragged the bleeding corpses into it. The frozen ground, the heavy snow, and the soldiers' lack of concern about the disposal of the bodies meant that the hole was not large enough to allow the earth to cover the dead. Some of the bodies lay on top of the ground. Then apparently the terrible pressures of the march and the weather and the bushwhacking and the murders burst through the control of one soldier. N.B.D. Jay, a Virginian attached to the Sixty-fourth, jumped on the pile of bodies and cried out, "Pat Juba for me, while I dance the damned scoundrels down to and through hell." Later the soldiers threw a little more earth on top of the grave and moved on. The next day when the families found the dead, they discovered that wild hogs had rooted up one man's body and eaten part of his head off.[24]

23. Ibid., especially *New York Times,* July 24, 1863. The killings are briefly mentioned in John Preston Arthur, *Western North Carolina: A History (from 1730 to 1913)* (Raleigh, N.C.: Edwards & Broughton, 1914), 603; Barrett, *Civil War in North Carolina,* 197, 198; Cotton, "Appalachian North Carolina," 119. Ellis, *Thrilling Adventures,* 408–20, has a more extended and imaginative account.

24. *New York Times,* July 24, 1863; *New York Herald,* July 24, 1863; *Memphis Bulletin,* July 15, 1863. All these accounts are the same except for the *Bulletin's* addition of a comment about the horribleness of the killings.

5

AFTERMATH

No greater disgrace can befall the army and through it our whole people, than the perpetuation of barbarous outrages upon the innocent and defenseless. Such proceedings not only disgrace the perpetrators and all connected with them, but are subversive of discipline and efficiency of the army, and destructive of the ends of our movement.

ROBERT E. LEE, June 1863

Shelton Laurel, home of Unionist mountaineers, refuge for loyalist guerrillas, had now been punished. Terror had demonstrated that this war was earnest, inescapable. There was no place to hide. Keith, Allen, and the soldiers of the Sixty-fourth had found some folks who deserved killing. Thirteen men, ages thirteen to sixty, lay piled together in a ditch in the snow. And the soldiers moved on. When they had gone, the families took the bodies from the ditch and carried them up a hillside and buried all of them side by side. They had all been kin while alive, all part of the integrated comradeship of the place, and now they would lie in death together.[1]

The price of this terror was enormously high for the killers too. They believed that some people deserved to die, but a couple of people they killed had almost been children, not to mention the women they had tortured. They could not keep quiet about this. Word of what had happened spread rapidly throughout the region. A.S.

---

1. The kinship of the victims was revealed to me by Mrs. Paul Wallin Shelton, April 4, 1977, in interview in Shelton Laurel.

Merrimon, seeking information on the killings, quickly got eyewitness accounts. Union spies, operating out of Tennessee and Kentucky, heard graphic accounts of the torture of old and young women and detailed descriptions of the victims' pleas for mercy. Men usually known for their reserve and restraint now could not be silent about what they had seen and perhaps done or maybe, even worse, had not tried to stop.[2]

While some of the killers were haunted by guilt, the state authorities responded with outrage. "Humanity revolts at such a crime," Merrimon wrote, and Governor Vance agreed: "barberous conduct . . . a scene of horror." Keith was "a disgrace to the service and to North Carolina." W.W. Holden, editor of the state's leading newspaper, roared against this "cowardly and wicked act," this "cold blooded murder," this "butchery," "In the name of outraged humanity we demand the punishment of the officer who is guilty of these murders."[3]

Not everyone was appalled by what had happened. Neighbors of Keith and Allen in Marshall believed that it was simple justice to show no mercy to such brutal marauders. One of the officers of the Sixty-fourth later justified the killing of these "audacious and vicious bushwhackers" by insisting that "only severe measures" would stop their cowardly harassment. Shortly after the *Raleigh Standard* trumpeted Holden's views, a correspondent from the mountains replied. The victims were, in fact, "thieves and robbers" who, for at least a year, had been killing, stealing, and forcing women and children "to strip off their clothes" in the dead of winter. Boys as young as ten had engaged in these outrages and were "the most active rogues in [the] company." To sympathize with such outlaws only encouraged more of their cruelties.[4]

2. Merrimon to Vance, Feb. 16, 1863, *OR,* ser. 1, vol. 18, 881. Merrimon described his information as coming from "one who got his information from *some* of the guilty parties" (my italics). Ellis, *Thrilling Adventures,* 408. Ellis claimed that his informant was "an eyewitness and one of the party." *Memphis Bulletin,* July 15, 1863. The source of this story was Colonel Robert Crawford who had learned of the massacre from someone who had written the information down "on the spot."

3. *Raleigh Standard,* March 18, 1863; Vance to Seddon, Feb. 28, 1863, *OR,* ser. 1, vol. 18, 897–98; Merrimon to Vance, Jan. 31, 1863, Governors Papers, North Carolina State Archives, Raleigh, N.C.

4. Letter from "Elbert," *Raleigh Standard,* April 22, 1863; B.T. Morris, "Sixty-fourth Regiment," in Walter Clark, ed., *Histories,* 661; Gaston, *Partisan Campaigns,* 26–27.

Yet power lay in the hands of those who sought to punish the kill-ers, not to praise them, and the officers and men who had hunted and killed the "Tories" and "bushwhackers" began to feel the force of vengeance themselves. Whatever people like Vance, Merrimon, and Holden felt about the need to stop Unionists in the western North Carolina mountains—and they were outspoken about it— now they had to show that the cause for which they fought and their own personal characters did not condone atrocity. They had to show themselves as well as others that the way they fought could not disgrace the cause they fought for. And they had to show that there was a limit, that they would and could create a limit, on the brutal-ity of war. Of course, they could not help the victims of Shelton Laurel, but they could stop there being more victims. And so those who fought guerrilla brutality with terror had to pay.

To some extent this decision was pragmatic as well as moral. Not only was the murder of helpless prisoners a sin, it was also what la-ter men would call counterproductive. Terror did not paralyze guer-rillas; it gave them power. It sanctified their marauding by hoisting over it the banner of betrayed and brutalized innocence. It ennobled the guerrilla's cause.[5]

The "Tory" bands in surrounding mountains were hardly affected by the Shelton Laurel killings. By the summer of 1863, residents of the region were writing to Vance in large numbers pleading for pro-tection from the outlaws. Reports noted that Confederates were killed at their homes, cabins were raided, and crops destroyed or taken. And when the Union army took Knoxville in September of the year, the Unionist mountaineers became even bolder, raiding towns, shooting into courthouses and jails, sweeping down on Rebel soldiers who were taking prisoners to jail, releasing the pris-oners, and then challenging the men of the home guard to come out and fight. They even took to drilling their forces in the open. Their

5. On the wisdom of using terror to subdue guerrillas, see Heilbrunn, *Partisan Warfare,* 143–57, and Robert D. Powers, Jr., "Guerrillas and the Laws of Wars," in Krulak, ed., *Studies in Guerrilla Warfare,* 22–28. Heilbrunn points out that even the Nazis learned the folly of summary execution of guerrillas. Powers's study is an offi-cial publication of the U.S. military, suggesting that even those engaged in the busi-ness of winning guerrilla wars know the limits of terror as a weapon. There was a long-standing maxim of warfare known to nineteenth-century military theorists that "*les represailles sont toujours inutiles.*" See Walter Laqueur, *Guerrilla: A Historical and Critical Study* (London: Weidenfeld, 1977), 124.

power was so great as almost to invite Federal soldiers to move into North Carolina. For a time the Confederates were able to block some of the passes leading from Tennessee, but their control was only temporary, as Union forces increasingly were seen operating in and through the mountains. One Union officer, George Kirk, was able to bring a force of from 150–300 men through the mountains to attack Morgantown, about seventy-five miles inside North Carolina itself. And by April 1864 the Unionist raiders and local "bushwhackers" were active throughout the mountains, and Colonel Kirk was operating out of the Shelton Laurel.[6]

Even as events were demonstrating the tactical folly of the murders, the authorities were moving to punish the murderers. Vance ordered Merrimon to prepare for a vigorous prosecution. In addition, the governor wrote to Secretary of War James Seddon urgently requesting an investigation, sending materials that named Keith as the responsible officer. The machinery of justice was rolling, but two factors were also combining that might slow it down or stop it completely. The first of these was the law regulating the relationship between military and civil justice. The second was the natural inclination of the Confederate army to avoid being spattered with an outrage.

The Confederate army operated, as did the Union, under the 1806 Articles of War. These articles reflected the traditional American suspicion of military power. They were designed to protect the power of civil courts even as they provided rules for the administration of military justice. The most fundamental way to protect civil justice was to limit the jurisdiction of military courts, both as to whom they could try and as to the crimes they could punish. Only people in the military or closely attached to it, such as sutlers, could be prosecuted. And these soldiers' courts had no jurisdiction over major felonies. Murder, manslaughter, arson, rape, robbery, and larceny all were under the control of civilian justice. The army could not lawfully try Keith and his accomplices for murder. They had to be tried by the North Carolina state courts. In March of 1863 the

6. J. Metcalf to Vance, July 6, 1863; J.J. Reynolds to Vance, July 12, 1863; W.C. Wallin to Vance, July 27, 1863; "Citizens of Western North Carolina" to Vance, July 29, 1863; Governors Papers, North Carolina State Archives. Barrett, *Civil War in North Carolina,* 199–201, 232–43.

Union army would adopt a new regulation that allowed military courts to try soldiers for these felonies. The Confederate army did not change its rules.[7]

If the law required that soldiers be tried for murder by civilian courts, it also demanded that the military assist these courts in apprehending and prosecuting them. Article 33 of the Articles of War said in plain language that when a soldier or officer was accused of a capital crime or of committing an offense against the person or property of any citizen of the nation, that soldier's commander and the officers of his regiment were to "use their utmost endeavors" to capture and deliver the accused to the civil magistrates. If these officers "willfully neglect[ed] or . . . refuse[d]" to do so, they would be "cashiered."

This was the direct command under which the army was to help civilians in punishing soldiers guilty of murder. However, a commander so inclined might punish an offender by discovering an offense that fell under military jurisdiction. The actions of the Sixty-fourth blossomed with such offenses. Article 32 gave the commander the power to court-martial any officer or soldier who beat or ill-treated any person or citizen of the United States. In fact, an officer who failed to punish an offender could himself be court-martialed. Presumably, whipping and temporary hanging fit this category of offenses.[8]

There was also a chance that the soldiers could be punished for a violation of "the customs of war." The possibility that the Shelton Laurel victims were guerrillas and, under the customs of war, could be summarily executed made such punishment problematic, but a vigilant commander might certainly have explored it.

A commander involved in other activities, however, a man lacking the heart to pursue a prosecution, might be able to comply half-heartedly with the law and hence throw the burden of prosecution back on civil authorities. Conditions in East Tennessee, particularly the constant change in commands, ensured that this possibility

7. William Winthrop, *Military Law and Precedents*, vol. 2 (Boston: Little, Brown, 1896), 1032–33; William M. Robinson, Jr., *Justice in Grey, A History of the Judicial System of the Confederate States of America* (New York: Russell and Russell, 1941), 359–82.
8. Winthrop, *Military Law and Precedents*, vol. 2, 1513.

would mature into a probability. As one commander replaced the other in that revolving chair, each could pass the responsibility on to his successor. It was not his job anymore, and he was probably happy to be able to wash his hands of it. And commanders came to this post with their minds on getting away as soon as possible. No one ever felt that East Tennessee was a permanent, personal responsibility. It was thus likely that the nastier aspects of the command might simply be ignored. Dealing with the ambiguities and viciousness of mountain warfare was a messy business at best, and there were things that a commander, even a highly moral one, especially a highly moral one, had better leave untouched. A new commander, faced with a myriad of new duties and with new relationships with inferiors, superiors, and civilian leaders to establish, might be inspired to lower the priority of this tar baby.

The army investigation into the actions of the Sixty-fourth proceeded in a way that revealed the touchiness of the issue. Just enough was done to give the illusion of activity, but not enough was done to stain the army with the blood of Shelton Laurel. The action, in fact, smelled of cover up, and that cover up reached to the office of the Confederate secretary of war.

As the investigation began, it appeared that the officers of the Sixty-fourth were feeling justice hurrying near. Governor Vance had asked Seddon to begin the investigation in late February, and by the end of that month a Captain Deaver of the Sixty-forth had been relieved of command. By mid-April three more junior officers had appeared before the investigatory boards. Two of them offered their resignations; the other was relieved of command. For a time, all four of these men remained in the army awaiting action by their superiors. Meanwhile, James A. Keith had to be dealt with. He had commanded at Shelton Laurel. He had been named in all the materials that Vance sent to the secretary of war as the person responsible for the killing there. By April 1863 the North Carolina newspapers had announced Keith's guilt and were calling for his head. A military investigation was gathering affidavits by witnesses testifying to the brutality of the Laurel raid as well as to the murders. There seemed to be no way that the army could avoid being involved in at least assisting the prosecution of one of its officers for a heinous crime. Also, given Keith's documented assertion that Henry Heth had ordered the killing, the prosecution could conceivably implicate a general, one who was known to be a friend of Robert E. Lee.[9]

The army, however, like a great beast, instinctively was trying to squirm away from responsibility for what had happened in Shelton Laurel. Vance waited for over two months for a report from Secretary Seddon on what had been found. Then on May 18 word came not from the secretary but from Merrimon. He had heard that Keith was going to escape their clutches. The colonel had been court-martialed, allowed to resign, and was going to run to where no one could find him. Immediately Vance wrote to Seddon, demanding a response.

Finally the secretary replied. Unfortunately, he wrote, Keith was gone. He would not be, could not be, punished by the army for the Shelton Laurel murders. He had not been held for civilian prosecution. Seddon's report was a jumble of contradiction and evasion. In the first place, he told Vance, no proceedings of the court-martial had been sent to him. Having thus relieved himself of having full knowledge of what the investigation had revealed, Seddon went on to announce the astounding fact that this investigation had not been into Keith's responsibility for the murders. Apparently the adjutant and the inspector general had not been aware of the Shelton Laurel murders when they were investigating Keith. He thus had been found guilty of an unspecified offense and allowed to resign. More than that, Keith himself had been permitted to announce the reason for his resignation: "the state of feeling existing between the officers of my regiment is such as to destroy my usefulness." Having written these words, James A. Keith was allowed to ride out of Knoxville and to vanish into the mountains.[10]

Despite an investigation into the massacre that had begun at least by early March, an investigation ordered by Seddon himself, despite a mass of testimony showing the atrocity, and despite the legal requirement that the army assist in apprehending soldiers guilty of murder, Keith was not even held by the army after his resignation. The Shelton Laurel murders were clearly in Seddon's mind, however,

9. Military Records of A.M. Deaver, William Keith, Thomas Keith, and S.E. Erwin, Military Records of the 64th North Carolina, Record Group 109, National Archives, Washington, D.C.

10. Merrimon to Vance, May 18, 1863; Thomas Ruffin, Jr., to Vance, June 15, 1863; Vance Papers, North Carolina State Archives, Raleigh, N.C.; Vance to Seddon, May 18, 1863; Seddon to Vance, May 23, 1863; *OR,* ser. 2, vol. 5, 956; Military Record of James A. Keith, Record Group 109, National Archives.

for in the very letter in which he told Vance of Keith's resignation, the secretary also told the governor that Keith and two witnesses had implicated General Heth in the killings. Despite this evidence, Keith was still at large, and on the same day that Seddon wrote to Vance, Henry Heth, now in Lee's Army of Northern Virginia, was promoted to major general.[11]

With the Keith problem disposed of, the four junior officers of the Sixty-fourth, who had been awaiting final disposition of their cases, were allowed to resign. There is no evidence to suggest the specific reasons for their resignations. Perhaps they suffered from that same mysterious failing that Seddon had refused to describe to Vance in reporting on the Keith investigation.

Unlike his cohorts, Lawrence Allen remained in the army for more than a year and a half after the murders. He was never court-martialed and never received any punishment by the military, even though the evidence collected on the Shelton Laurel killings implicated him as well. Somehow it was possible for the army to quarantine the massacre investigation so that it did not infect its regular operations.

Allen was, however, in trouble with the army on other grounds. By midsummer 1863, Governor Vance had uncovered his substitute racket. Whether Allen skimmed excess profit for himself as a broker between buyer and substitutes, or provided as substitutes men who were unfit, or extorted money from men he threatened to draft is not clear. What is clear is that he made a profit of over $20,000 in this business and that Confederate officers were not supposed to make money supplying soldiers for their own army.[12]

Seeing how easily Keith had avoided punishment, Allen apparently tried to resign when he discovered that his racket had been found out. This time Vance was not going to let his man escape, and he wrote to Seddon urgently requesting that Allen not be allowed to resign. The "honor of my state" demanded that Allen be put on trial for his conduct, and apparently the governor believed that a military trial would exact the proper punishment.

The colonel was brought before a court-martial in August 1863,

11. Morrison, ed., *Memoirs of Henry Heth,* xliv; Military Records of Deaver, Keith, Keith, and Erwin.

12. Mitchell, *Legal Aspects of Conscription and Exemption in North Carolina,* 18–22; Albert Moore, *Conscription and Conflict in the Confederacy,* 27–51.

found guilty, and punished. Again, however, the army lashed its officers half-heartedly. Allen's penalty was suspension without pay for six months. This was the same penalty he had received a year earlier when he had reported as present a soldier who was on private business away from camp. And now, if Vance was right about Allen's earnings, the colonel would hardly be injured by the loss of pay.[13]

Furthermore, his suspension seems to have had little effect on his military activities. Allen stayed with the remnants of his unit after the main body had been captured at Cumberland Gap in September. He was with them throughout the fall and winter of 1863, chasing bushwhackers and attacking and capturing alleged Union recruiters operating in the mountains. Perhaps at this time he remembered Shelton Laurel, for in later years he insisted that the recruiters he captured "were treated as prisoners of war and sent to Asheville."[14]

The lightness of his "punishment" seems to have convinced Allen that he had little to fear from the military. There was, of course, still his old zest for action and for making a reputation for himself. At the end of his suspension he asked for reassignment. He had gathered together about a hundred men and he wanted to join General John H. Morgan, the cavalry raider who specialized in daring raids behind enemy lines. Allen's hopes were dashed when his request was denied. So on June 3, 1864, he resigned from the army and sought other adventures for himself. By the next year he was off to Arkansas, seeking in that state's mountains a place and station like that he had in Marshall.[15]

As for Keith, who was now free of military justice, he faced a much greater threat from civilians. Vance had promised that "I will follow him [Keith] to the gates of hell, or hang him" and instructed Merrimon to do everything possible to capture, try, and punish the fugitive.[16]

The former colonel thus became the object of a hunt. He was forced to retreat into the mountains, to hide, and to seek friends,

13. Vance to Seddon, Aug. 13, 1863, Military Record of L.M. Allen, Record Group 109, National Archives, Washington, D.C.

14. Military Record of L.M. Allen; Gaston, *Partisan Campaigns* 12–15; Morris, "Sixty-fourth Regiment," 663–64, 671.

15. Military Record of L.M. Allen; Gaston, *Partisan Campaigns,* 19–25.

16. W.K. Boyd, ed., *Memoirs of W.W. Holden* (Durham, N.C., Seeman Printery, 1911), 27–28; Merrimon to Vance, May 29, 1863, Vance Papers, State Archives, Raleigh, N.C.

food, and shelter in isolated cabins and caves, sometimes sleeping out at night for fear of being caught, avoiding strangers, fleeing men on horseback. The man who had separated himself from the wilderness now tried to become as much a part of it as he could. Meanwhile, all around him enemies grew and prospered. Increasing numbers of Union army recruiters appeared in the mountains. George Kirk again moved through the high passes to raid North Carolina's upper piedmont region. "Tories" and "bushwhackers" and deserters openly and boldly displayed their burgeoning power.[17]

As the fugitive Keith hid and watched Unionism gathering strength, he was assailed from the other side by the law of Confederate North Carolina. Merrimon organized the prosecution against him. The army bestirred itself finally to order witnesses from the Sixty-Fourth to Marshall, where the trial would be held, if they could catch the accused. The president of the military court in Knoxville sent affidavits to Vance containing testimony from eyewitnesses of the massacre. Keith, however, kept eluding his captors. From time to time someone would see him in the mountains, but never long enough to take him prisoner. Witnesses would be gathered in the hope that the sheriff would find him. Despite these efforts throughout 1863-64, Keith remained at large.[18]

As the war moved to its close, state authorities had their attention diverted to other matters. Increasing Union victories, antagonism between Vance and Confederate President Davis over the use of North Carolina soldiers, growing inflation, mounting casualties — all deflated enthusiasm among Tarheels for the rebellion. A peace movement gathered force, energized by claims from W.W. Holden that it was "a rich man's war and a poor man's fight." The 1864 election featured a contest between Vance and Holden for the governor's chair. Vance's victory did little to save the state from its fate. Fort Fisher, protecting North Carolina's seacoast, fell in January 1865. William Sherman's terrible army advanced from Charleston, and General George Stoneman advanced through the western mountains and marched throughout the upper piedmont, destroying railroads and bridges. The state government collapsed.

17. Barrett, *Civil War in North Carolina,* 199–201, 232–43.
18. Thomas Ruffin, Jr., to Vance, June 15, 1863; A.S. Merrimon to Vance, July 31, 1863; Merrimon to Vance, September 18, 1863; Vance Papers, State Archives, Raleigh, N.C.

The death of Vance's government brought no relief to Keith. Although Confederates could no longer chase him, Union soldiers did, and as the war was ending, they caught him. He was placed in prison in Castle Pinckney. He stayed there for eight months, was taken to Raleigh, and then to Marshall, where justice, or at least vengeance, waited. Victory, unlike defeat, which counseled forgetfulness, gave mountain Unionists impetus to remember their sufferings and the power to exact retribution. In November 1865 prominent northern journalist Whitelaw Reid found mountaineers with searing memories of the war. "Men who had been driven from their homes or half starved in the mountains, or hunted for with dogs, were not likely to be very gentle in their treatment of the men who persecuted them; and one readily believed what all observers said, that in no place in the South had the bitterness of feeling, engendered by the war been so intense, or the violence so bloody in its consequence." As one mountain Confederate told Reid (whom he had mistaken for a southerner) when they approached Knoxville, "This isn't good country for you and me. They're all tories here, every damned scoundrel of them. I've been chased off from my home because I had been in the Confederate army. For three weeks now I've dodged about in the woods, and now I'm going to get out of this Yankee country."[19]

While mountain Unionists nursed their vengeance, others in the state sought forgetfulness, a way to douse the hatred and reconcile the bitterness born of four years of war. The state legislative session of 1866–67, guided by moderates (old Whigs who had opposed secession but fought with their state after Sumter), gave a strong answer to the vengeful. In December 1866 they passed a law granting "full and complete amnesty, pardon, and discharge" to all officers and soldiers of either Union or Confederate armies who in the course of duty, or under the order of a superior, committed "any homicides, felonies, or misdemeanors." Furthermore, anyone accused of these crimes would be assumed to have been acting under

19. *North Carolina Weekly Standard,* Feb. 24, 1869; Whitelaw Reid, *After the War: A Tour of the Southern States, 1865-1866* (New York: Moore, Wilslach and Baldwin, 1866), 350-52. See also Andrews, *The South Since the War,* 113-16. For evocation of the bitterness of the mountain feeling against Confederates, see William Faulkner, "Mountain Victory," in *Collected Stories of William Faulkner* (New York: Modern Library, 1948), 745-80.

orders unless the contrary could be proven. Also, recognizing that the war had absorbed civilians as well as soldiers, the legislators swept this amnesty and pardon over private citizens who "for preservation of their lives or property, or for the protection of their families, associated themselves together for the preservation of law and order."[20]

The state supreme court joined this rush to murder postwar revenge in its cradle. Within days of the passage of the amnesty act, judges decided a case involving the prosecution of Federal soldiers for wounding members of the home guard in a mountain skirmish. Deciding that the act had eliminated the need to prosecute, the court took the occasion to lecture Tarheels on the benefits of turning the other cheek.

The war, Justice Edwin G. Reade argued, had troubled society "to its deep foundations." People who were now neighbors had fought each other, destroying property and lives. And "those who were in command had to compel obedience, and were sometimes too imperious; those who had to serve were worn out and irritable, and sometimes resistant; the rapacious plundered and the innocent suffered." Such an environment taxed the legal system beyond its strength. Justice in individual cases was impossible to extract from the "exaggerations of irritating facts, the conflict of witnesses, the discussion between zealous advocates, the denunciations of parties." To try, convict, and punish all the individual cases "would not only keep alive these evils, but would cause them to spread into a pestilence. While so many have injuries to revenge, quite as many have errors to regret . . . it will be a great public good if the past can be forgiven and forgotten."[21]

Despite these sentiments and despite a law sweeping enough probably to provide amnesty even for his crime, Keith remained in jail. No one sued out a writ of *habeas corpus* to free him under the amnesty act. Legislators and judges in Raleigh might proclaim forgiveness, but no one with influence in the mountains was ready to forgive Keith. As the state fought out its battles over reconstruction, as

20. Law quoted in *State v. William Blalock and Others,* 61 *North Carolina Reports,* 249–50; J.G. deRoulac Hamilton, *Reconstruction in North Carolina* (New York: Columbia Univ. Press, 1914) 182–90. Indicative of its conservative temper, this legislature also rejected the proposed Fourteenth Amendment.

21. *State v. Blalock,* 248–49.

it moved from provisional military government to civil government, to military reconstruction and back to civil government again, Keith stayed in jail. None of these governments had sympathy for his plight. Certainly no state official who curried President Andrew Johnson's favor could afford to help him. Johnson was a mountain Unionist from Greeneville, Tennessee, less than a day's ride from Shelton Laurel. And W.W. Holden, provisional governor under Johnson and then under congressional Reconstruction, had no sympathy either. Even moderate civilian Governor Jonathan Worth was not interested in freeing the colonel. In a state plagued by the guerrilla violence of the Ku Klux Klan, perhaps the idea of letting Keith loose was too much.

By the time he came to trial, the colonel had spent up to twenty-six months in jail. Nevertheless, memories were long in Madison County, and when his trial finally began in December of 1868, Keith's lawyers moved for and got a change of venue from Madison to Buncombe County. This maneuver perhaps ensured a more sympathetic jury, but it did nothing to mollify the prosecutors. They were not in a forgiving mood.

Keith was indicted, not once for all thirteen murders, but thirteen individual times, for each of the killings. When an Asheville jury acquitted him on December 9, 1868, of the killing of one of the victims, the court gave the traditional incantation that he was to be discharged and "go hence without delay." Keith did not go anywhere, however, because the next day he was charged with a second murder and the day after with a third.[22]

When the next day came and Keith again was brought into court, his lawyers had finally discovered the amnesty act. Surely here was his passport to freedom; however, an obstacle loomed. In 1868 the Reconstruction constitutional convention, mandated under the 1867 Congressional Reconstruction Act, had written a provision that possibly wiped out that amnesty. "[All] indictments which shall have been found, or may hereinafter be found, for any crime or offense committed before this Constitution takes effect," the key provision said, "may be proceeded upon in the proper Courts, but no punishment may be inflicted which is forbidden by this Constitution."[23]

22. Buncombe County (N.C.) Superior Court, Docket Book, Fall Term 1868, December 9-11, 1868, 426-27.
23. *State v. Keith,* 63 *North Carolina Reports,* 140-45.

Had the 1868 constitution snatched Keith's amnesty from him? That was the issue that would bring the soldier's case to the state supreme court. His lawyers claimed that amnesty was irreversible. The district court judge held that the state constitution destroyed the amnesty. Keith's counsel appealed. The prosecutors agreed to merge a total of seven counts of murder into this one case and take the issue to Raleigh.[24]

When the case took this form, the mountaineers would have been justified in believing that by some legerdemain the lawyers in Asheville and Raleigh had managed to forget the only questions worth considering: Had Keith killed people who deserved killing? Did Keith himself deserve killing? The system of law was somehow replacing the code of community justice. A simple question was being smothered in subtlety. Which law, that of the 1866 legislature or that of the 1868 constitution, prevailed in an apparent clash between them? More subtle than that, did the later constitution itself, in its stated devotion to "due process of law," its prohibition of *ex post facto* laws, undermine its own declaration that existing indictments would continue in effect?

These were the sort of games in which sophistry paralyzed confrontation with issues of right and wrong. To mountain Unionists the crime of Shelton Laurel, the *sin* of Shelton Laurel was there. The 1866 legislature could not change it, the 1868 convention could not change it, and the judges could not change it.

Perhaps they would have been comforted to know that if the issue before the state supreme court had been Keith's guilt or innocence, it is likely that he would have lost. Since no one doubted that Keith had commanded in the Shelton Laurel or that he had given the order to fire, the key issue affecting his guilt was whether there was an excuse for the killings. Was he excused by the orders of General Heth, by the ongoing, pervasive brutality of mountain warfare? Had the victims lost the right to be treated as prisoners of war by engaging in guerrilla activities? The probable answers to these questions would have given Keith no comfort.

The mere fact of a military order did not allow a man to forget his moral obligations, his humanity. Keith himself had not been in a position where pressures on him would have justified forgetting that

24. Ibid.

fact. He had not been threatened with death for failure to obey. The best possible defense for him was that killing of prisoners was such a common occurrence that he assumed that an order to do so was lawful. This clearly was not the case. Other prisoners in the same roundup had gone to jail, not to their deaths. Another justification for the killings was that guerrillas forfeited the right to be treated as prisoners of war and, if caught, might be shot on sight. International law supported this contention on the condition that the guerrillas be clearly engaged in guerrilla activities when taken. The Shelton Laurel victims had not been so engaged. They had been taken while at home and where was the evidence that they were guerrillas? Further destructive of Keith's position was an opinion rendered in 1865 by United States Attorney General James Speed for President Andrew Johnson. Speed told Johnson that whatever the status of guerrillas caught in the act of depredations or fighting regular soldiers, men captured and held by soldiers in other circumstances might not be summarily killed. Considering the awful power that international law gave over guerrillas, it was especially important that military tribunals, not individual summary judgment, determine their guilt. A commander who acted otherwise, Speed advised, "would become a mere butcher of men."[25]

All these issues were ignored in *State v. Keith*. The only question the North Carolina supreme court dealt with was whether a provision of a later constitution could destroy an act of amnesty. The answer was no. William Blackstone, John Marshall, the constitution of North Carolina itself, and the United States Constitution, not to mention "great principles . . . inseparable from American government and [which] follow the American flag," all these said that Keith should go free. The article of the constitution that attacked the amnesty was an *ex post facto* law. Justice proscribed it. "We think," the court said, "the Judge should have discharged the prisoner."[26]

On a fundamental question amnesty, forgetfulness, had won. The 1866 law lived, despite the 1868 constitutional provision. The highest court in the state had overruled the local judge. Yet Keith did not

---

25. *Opinions of the Attorney General of the United States,* vol. 11 (1865), 307–308; *State v. Cook, North Carolina Supreme Court Reports,* vol. 61, 518; Wheaton, *Elements of International Law,* 406. See also Francis Lieber, "Guerrilla Parties," in *Miscellaneous Writings,* vol. 2, 277–92.

26. *State v. Keith,* 144–45.

go free, for the supreme court had left open the door to further prosecutions. Justice William B. Rodman had observed that while the transcript of the trial in Asheville did mention more than one indictment, the only case that the court was deciding was the single indictment of Keith for the murder of Roderick ("Stob Rod") Shelton. This suggested that Keith could still be tried for the eleven remaining murders.

In each of these remaining indictments all the facts were the same; only the victims differed. Keith's lawyers could plead that the amnesty law covered him on every indictment. What gave that argument special force was the fact that the prosecutors, in order to get the issue of amnesty law versus constitutional provision decided, had conceded that Keith's actions in Shelton Laurel were covered under the 1866 act.

The prosecutors did have a possible line of attack, however. They could urge in each case that the amnesty law covered only "homicides and felonies . . . done in the discharge of duties." They could argue that the murder of prisoners was not covered because there could be no duty to perform a manifestly unlawful act. Back in 1863 Merrimon had made this exact argument to Vance. "I do not suppose they had any order to do such a barbarous deed," he wrote, "but if they had, the order was void absolutely, no matter by whom issued." This contention might still be made before eleven successive juries, assuming that the prosecutors could frame their indictment in such a way as to finesse *State v. Keith.* If not, Keith's lawyers could throw that case in their faces before the trial was minutes old and no jury would hear anything because the trial judge would be bound by the state supreme court decision. He would have to dismiss the case.[27]

Because of the obstacles posed by the state's concession, it would take an especially vigilant and inspired prosecutor to continue the prosecution of Keith. The inspiration was there. Despite *State v. Keith,* prosecutors filed five more indictments against him for the murders in the Shelton Laurel.

Despite decisions of judges in Raleigh, despite laws passed by faraway legislators, there were people in the mountains who still wanted

27. Merrimon to Vance, Jan. 31, 1863, Governors Papers, State Archives, Raleigh, N.C.

revenge. They were not impressed by the rhetoric of lawyers. They were not awed by "amnesty" or "*ex post facto.*" They were un-swayed by "John Marshall," "principles of American Government," or "the American flag." Even the acquittal of Keith for one of the murders did not deter them. Perhaps they felt that the cosmopolitan jurors of Asheville had simply released one of their own. The mountain avengers would not seek amnesia from the brutality of war; they would bring Keith the punishment he deserved.

The prisoner himself surely doubted that he deserved punishment. He had killed "bushwhackers" and "Tories," men who fired from ambush, who robbed and murdered loyal Confederates. Marauders did not carry their birth certificates with them. They did carry rifles that killed and maimed, no matter what was the age of the finger on the trigger. Now he had stayed in jail for over two years, his wife was without her husband, his children without their father. His enemies were still determined to destroy him. Finally he had enough of being the victim of such injustice. On the night of February 21, 1869, a few days before his vindication by the state supreme court, he escaped from the Buncombe County jail in Asheville and vanished from North Carolina. For the next two years the authorities ordered his arrest, but he was not found. On June 26, 1871, the state dropped its prosecution.[28]

The Shelton Laurel killings did not become a major incident of the Civil War. A few newspapers picked up the story after the *Memphis Bulletin* broke it in July 1863, but little public outcry followed. Perhaps the ongoing brutality of mountain warfare taught people to believe that war was like that and maybe the victims deserved killing anyway. Apologists for Keith spoke of the conditions of guerrilla warfare, of the brutality of the bushwhackers. His friends hid him from the authorities for over two years. A jury of his peers, in the one chance they had to express their feelings officially, found him not guilty of the killings.[29]

On the national scene the thirteen deaths were quickly overwhelmed by mountains of dead. Fredericksburg, Chancellorsville, Gettysburg—what possible meaning was there in thirteen murders

28. Buncombe County (N.C.) Superior Court, Docket Book, Spring, Fall 1869, 1870; Spring 1871; *North Carolina Weekly Standard,* March 10, 1869.
29. Ibid.

in the midst of what Whitman called "this slaughterhouse"? Even in the category of guerrilla warfare, Shelton Laurel was quickly surpassed. Less than a month after the North Carolina killings gained national attention, William C. Quantrill and Lawrence, Kansas, shocked public consciousness with the story of 155 murders — ten times the killings that had happened in the Laurels.

Only North Carolina remembered, perhaps because Zeb Vance was from the mountains, perhaps because the Holden administration that followed Vance wanted to sustain its Unionist support in the west. But whatever the motives of governors in Raleigh for remembering, the mountain people themselves had better reasons.

In 1864 four Union soldiers escaping from Salisbury prison made their way to a place called Crab Orchard in East Tennessee. There they found a small cabin and, looking in the window, discovered it was occupied by two little girls and an old woman. Shivering from the cold, the escapees entered the cabin. The little girls crawled quickly out of sight. The old woman threw down her knitting and told them to get out — she had nothing to give them. They tried to explain their desperation to her, but she ignored them. The little girls finally crawled out into the room and explained that their grandma was deaf. Their mother would return soon. The men sat by the fire and waited.

When the mother returned, she was angry to find the men in her house. They had no right, she told them, and it was cruel to imperil the lives of her family by staying. "If Keith's Confederates dash in here and find you, they will kill you and us, and burn our home. Please go on, gentlemen, and Heaven will bless you. I am alone here, or you would not dare invade my home." The men begged to stay, assuring here there would be no danger. With tears in her eyes she relented. They could sleep that night in the barn. The next day they moved on.[30]

30. Drake, *Fast and Loose in Dixie*, 208-209.

EPILOGUE

*Praise the world to the Angel, not
the untellable: you can't impress him
with the splendoure you've felt; in
the cosmos where he more feelingly
feels you're only a tyro. So show
him some simple thing, remoulded
by age after age, till it lives in our
hands and eyes as part of ourselves.*
RAINER MARIA RILKE,
Duino Elegies

Heth, Keith, Allen, and the people of Shelton Laurel took separate paths away from the massacre. Heth left East Tennessee within a month after the event. Having applied for a transfer in November 1862, he must have been delighted to escape the mountain quicksand. He joined his friend and mentor Robert E. Lee and the Army of Northern Virginia. The two men would grow very close; Heth was the only general that Lee called by his first name. Their association was not always smooth, however, for Heth's generalship left much to be desired.

His flaws were not immediately revealed in Virginia. Heth's first major battle with Lee's army was Chancellorsville, where he demonstrated notable personal courage. Seriously wounded, he remained in command, refusing to be relieved until the Confederates had won. His service was distinguished enough to assist his promotion to major general.[1]

---

1. Morrison, ed., *Memoirs of Henry Heth,* xliv, 193–95; *OR,* ser. 1, vol. 25, pt. 1, 885–89, 916, 920.

117

Then came Gettysburg and again things began to go wrong. Heth commanded the division that first made contact with the enemy on June 30. His next move was to commit his entire division to an advance on the town the next morning. He committed his forces without any effort to determine just what sort of enemy force he was encountering. The result was 2,700 Confederate casualties within twenty-five minutes. The battle of Gettysburg was on.

As the defeated Confederate forces retreated from Pennsylvania and into Maryland, Heth commanded a rear guard and blundered again. This time he allowed a Union cavalry squadron to outflank one of his brigades and to take more than 225 prisoners. Then the battle of the Wilderness offered him another chance to show his failings and he made the most of it. After a day of fighting in terrain that guaranteed confusion, Heth's troops found themselves with their alignment destroyed, their organization in chaos. Instead of rectifying the situation, Heth left his men in this jumbled mess, risking disaster. "A moderately diligent corporal," one military historian notes, would have acted to restore order, but Heth did nothing. His men were saved from a brutal mauling only by the failure of Federal troops to move against the Rebels. To continue the catalog of mishaps, Heth would be reprimanded by Lee at Petersburg for neglect in preparing defense works.[2]

Heth's mistakes did not arise from a lack of courage. He had again been wounded in the Wilderness and fought bravely in struggles around Petersburg. Yet his virtues marked his defects. Personal courage, recklessness toward his own safety, revealed a man heedless of the consequences of his actions and unable to see what an enemy might do to counteract his moves. Solicitous of his subordinates' needs and welfare in immediate terms, he did not extend his concern to what he risked in their behalf by his own impulsiveness. The rash lieutenant who galloped recklessly after Mexican guerrillas became the captain who marched boldly, and vastly outnumbered, into Indian camps, and who threatened rock throwing Mormons with death. This man became the general who raged at the rangers and civilians of West Virginia and was robbed of his chance to let boldness win the day in Cincinnati. And this was the man who had allowed guerrilla warfare in North Carolina to spawn a massacre.

2. Morrison, *Memoirs of Heth,* xlv–lv, 193–94.

His career was of a piece: boldness, courage, recklessness, death for the soldiers he commanded, too often unnecessary death. The profession that was to be everything to him—a job, a career, a way of life—ended, often stained with failure. The good was too frequently overcome by the bad and somehow had to be, because the one was born of the other.[3]

Heth left the army and found little success in civilian life. A coal mining venture failed when he neglected to investigate carefully to see if the coal was of high enough quality to mine profitably. He failed as a life insurance agent when he ignored administrative details of the job—inquiries from the home office unanswered, policies allowed to lapse, client claims unprocessed. An effort to create a railroad company failed when a competing line got the Federal charter. Only from 1885–89 did Heth recapture the satisfaction and success he had known before the war. His connections with Secretary of the Interior L.Q.C. Lamar brought him an appointment as special agent for the Bureau of Indian Affairs. He traveled through scenes of earlier happiness, investigating complaints, inspecting Indian schools, suggesting improvements in agency administration. He threw himself into this work and showed concern for the Indians as well as the agency, reporting the outrageous cheating of a northwestern tribe and expressing admiration for Indians who seemed doomed to fall before the modern society of whites.[4]

In 1889 he retired from this post and lived out his life rather quietly, working as a Confederate representative on a War Department board set up to mark the battlefield at Sharpsburg. This gave him opportunities to make appearances at the erection of monuments and at the funerals of former Rebel leaders. He wrote his memoirs too—seeking to recapture in them not just the fighting but, more importantly, the social experience of army life. He recalled the pranks, the parties, the dinners, the good times he had with Burnside, Hancock, Grant, Lee, and the rest. He wrote about the battles too, of course, but more vivid was his description of his profession's way of life. His memoirs were a family album, an attempt to recall and recapture the world he had lost, a world that somehow, some-

3. Ibid., lvi–lviii. Douglas Southall Freeman evaluates Heth as unlucky, but James Morrison believes that Heth's own flaws explain most of his "bad luck." *Lee's Lieutenants,* vol. 3 (New York: Scribners, 1946), 507; Morrison, *Memoirs of Heth,* lvii.
4. Morrison, *Memoirs of Heth,* lix–lxiii.

time in the Civil War, had gone wrong. Heth died of Bright's disease in 1899.[5]

James Keith vanished from the North Carolina mountains after his escape. Two years in jail, a reputation for brutality that would span decades, surviving enemies who would never forgive—these destroyed any hope he may have had of reclaiming the bright days of 1860, of wealth, influence, vigor, hope. By the time of his escape he was forty-one, his daughter, Laura, was twelve, and his son, Douglas, was ten. His wife, Margaret, had grown into middle age with him. They left the place where once they seemed to have everything and tried to rebuild their lives. Keith may have hoped they could forget the price of what he had done. In 1871 he sold his land in Madison County through an attorney. He was last heard of in Arkansas. In 1879 a William Keith would be elected to the state legislature there for one term, but James A. Keith was gone.[6]

Like Keith, Lawrence Allen fled Madison County and left behind him property, friends, and influence. He and his wife, Polly, and their surviving child, Amy, moved to Arkansas. He settled in Benton County, a mountainous place in the northwestern corner of the state—much like the place he had left. Allen stayed out of politics, farmed for twenty years as his child grew up and he grew older, and forgot for a time what he had lost. In 1884 he moved to Colorado for a few months and then to Arizona, seeking a climate that would improve his declining health. There the past caught up with him.[7]

By chance he became acquainted with a man who, like himself, had been a colonel during the Civil War. The fact that "Colonel" Bell had fought for the Union probably only added to the warm satisfaction of their reminiscing. They stopped in a hotel one day for coffee and to recall the old days. At a table nearby sat another visitor, a Mr. Dill of New York. Dill had not forgiven the South for the sins of twenty-five years before. Overhearing the colonels' conversation, he began to interrupt with insults about secession, the South, Confederate leaders and soldiers. The two veterans tried to ignore him, but then Dill unleashed the ultimate insult. "The women

5. Ibid., 14–32, 41–49, 58–61, 71–72, 75–78, 112–13, 198–99, 209–10.
6. Wellman, *Kingdom of Madison,* 94, 209n; Fay Hempstead, *Pictorial History of Arkansas* (St. Louis: n.p., 1896), 1224.
7. The account of Allen in postwar years is based on Gaston, *Partisan Campaigns.*

of the South," he announced loudly, "were no better than the street-walkers of New York City."

Outrage! Blasphemy! Allen threw his hot coffee in the man's face, followed it with the sugar bowl, and demanded satisfaction on the field of honor. The day was set, Washington's Birthday 1885; the place, Sonora, Mexico; the weapons, Colt 45's at sixty feet. The night before the duel, Allen wrote a last letter, "To my friends throughout the Sunny South, and more especially my comrades, late in arms." He was a true son of the South, he told them, and had great respect for the true Federal soldier. He thanked Bell for acting as his second, and then came the ritual outpouring of a great heart: "God bless the ladies of the South! I well remember their self denial, their great energy and true devotion to the Southern Cause; their great grief at the loss of husbands, brothers, and friends during the great struggle between the States. There is not a lady of mature age who has not felt its pangs. All honor to them." On the morrow he would meet "this wanton traducer of the noble women of the South." He hoped he would "not be considered rash" for his act. The duel took place in Sonora. Allen was wounded, but presumably he saved the honor of southern womanhood, for Dill died of his wounds.

Allen did not destroy his "last letter." He set it aside, perhaps thinking that it might be useful to him someday. He returned to Arkansas and then in 1892 went back to Marshall. There he discovered that his enemies remained powerful. They had taken land that he still held in the county and sold it, allegedly for unpaid debts. When Allen protested, they responded by reviving the Shelton Laurel story. In reply the colonel helped a friend prepare a pamphlet with the modest title *Partisan Campaigns of Colonel Lawrence M. Allen Commanding the 64th Regiment, North Carolina Troops, During the Late Civil War. Valiant Deeds of Heroic Patriotism. Self Sacrifices for the Southern Cause. His Rapid Promotion. Terrific Contests with the Notorious Bushwhacker Kirk. Duel in Defense of the Honor of Southern Womanhood.* Included in it were stories of Allen's courage, energy, leadership, and intelligence. Special attention was given to his duel in Sonora, and the "last letter" was quoted in full.

The massacre itself was never mentioned directly. The pamphlet sought sympathy by detailing Allen's fights with Unionist "bushwhackers." Also detailed at length was the movement of the Sixty-fourth into the Laurel region and then the pathetic story of the deaths of his children. Never once did Allen come directly to grips with the killings in Shelton Laurel. He responded to his accusers in a general way, obliquely referring to their charges. He had never killed children, he insisted. There was, of course, the sixteen-year-old, Chandler, but he was "an armed and desperate outlaw." He did not mention David Shelton, age thirteen. Perhaps David had slipped his mind. Perhaps Allen was not ashamed of what he had done. He may even have been a little proud of it. He was willing to allow his friend to boast that "for twenty years after the war when their children were unruly, mothers in order to quiet them would tell them that 'Allen is coming with his soldiers.'" There were homes in Shelton Laurel where such words would have had an impact.

Unlike Heth, Keith, and Allen, who vainly sought a way of life that war had taken from them, the people of Shelton Laurel abided in their place. The blood of their kin had soaked the earth. Thirteen graves now marked a hillside halfway up their valley. But the war ebbed away, and life was permitted to flow on as it had before the war.

There remained, of course, hatreds that might be aroused in these mountains. In the 1870s conservatives in North Carolina, old secessionists and their allies, set out to undo the promises of equality that the war had brought. They sought to terrorize the freedmen and the old Unionists who supported them. Faced with a governor, W.W. Holden, who believed in protecting the blacks and their allies, the so-called Redeemers resorted to the vigilantism of the KKK. Midnight attacks, the burning of homes and farms, and the torture and killing of Unionists, white and black, took place throughout the state. Holden sought help in destroying the Klan and found it in the person of George Kirk, the Tennessee mountaineer who had led the Second and Third North Carolina regiments in the Union army. Kirk turned to the mountains to rally the old Unionists. Handbills circulated throughout the hills calling on supporters to revenge the blood of Unionists. Over six hundred mountaineers answered the call and swept through the state trying to put down Klan violence. Ultimately, Holden and Kirk and his men failed. Racism, war weariness, the governor's lack of restraint brought conservatives back to power. Nevertheless the response to Kirk's call showed the endurance of mountain Unionism.[8]

8. Hamilton, *Reconstruction in North Carolina,* 482–533, describes the details of

The support given Kirk and Holden in the mountains was only one manifestation of the war's impact on the politics of the region. Mountain Unionists could be enlisted to strike at wartime foes and at forces that seemed to challenge the victory of the Union. But securing the other major goal of Reconstruction, racial equality, posed a much more equivocal problem. Although mountaineers had hated slavery as an economic and political institution, they supported it as a method of race control, for they believed profoundly in the inferiority of blacks. Nationally known mountain Unionists like Brownlow and Johnson had defended slavery up to the issuance of the Emancipation Proclamation. Their support for the measure rested on a commitment to saving the Union, not to bringing racial equality to blacks.

Their constituents felt the same way, even after the war. Whitelaw Reid was told in Knoxville that the white Unionists were profoundly threatened by any effort to do more for blacks than release them from slavery. Blacks in the town were frequently killed for forgetting their place. "There was, I should judge, absolutely no public sentiment in favor of negro suffrage," Reid noted, "and scarcely any in favor of negro education. The prejudices against them were, with the most, intense; and if any way of driving them out of the country can be found, it will be very apt to be put into force. The freedmen have more hope from Virginia Rebels than from East Tennessee Loyalists, if the public sentiment of Knoxville may be accepted as a test. In this, as in all their other political feelings, the Mountaineers are fervidly in earnest." In 1865 John Trowbridge put the matter more succinctly: "East Tennesseans, though opposed to slavery and secession, do not like niggers." And a year later a Freedmen's Bureau official observed, "It is a melancholy fact that among the bitterest opponents of the negro in Tennessee are the intensely radical loyalists of the mountain districts."[9]

Yet Reconstruction forces made mountaineers and blacks politi-

---

the so-called Kirk-Holden war. His intense pro-conservative bias undermines an otherwise thorough work. A more balanced view is in Allan Trelease, *White Terror* (New York: Harper, 1971), 215-17. See also W. McKee Evans, *Ballots and Fence Rails, Reconstruction in the Lower Cape Fear* (New York: Norton, 1967), 146.

9. Reid, *After the War,* 352; John Trowbridge, *The South* (Hartford, Conn.: L. Stebbins, 1865), 239; *Report of the Joint Committee on Reconstruction* (Washington, D.C.: Government Printing Office), pt. 1, 122, 117, 121.

cal allies. War experiences made mountaineers supporters of the congressional policy of Reconstruction. Seeking vengeance against Rebels, they were dismayed when Andrew Johnson seemed to abandon them by pardoning Confederates and opposing measures that protected Unionists in the South. Mountaineers strongly favored disfranchisement of their enemies and began to organize for the Republican party, to protect themselves and to advance their interests.[10]

This political decision allied them with freedmen, who also sought protection from the Republican Congress against conservatives. Black ballots were necessary to elect friendly state politicians and so the mountaineers were reluctantly drawn to support equal suffrage. The latent racism of the mountain region, however, meant that white Republicans had to hedge their support and not go too far. Only a fact of demography made the alliance possible. Since there were very few blacks in the mountains, the consequences of expanding Negro rights would not be experienced directly by mountaineers. The strongest Republican districts in the South generally were those with the fewest blacks, and this generalization held true in the southern Appalachians as well.[11]

The potency of mountain racism is suggested by the fact that despite the scarcity of blacks in the mountains, measures that seemed too favorable to Negroes brought defeats to the Republicans. When Congress passed the KKK acts in 1870 and 1871, Democrats were able to allege that Republicans in Washington were going to meddle with race relations in southern counties. And when Congress passed the 1875 Civil Rights bill, which permitted integrated schools and mandated integrated public accommodations, the lid blew off in a massive reaction. Republicans lost even in their strongest mountain districts, those of East Tennessee. In 1868 mountain Republicans had won almost 62 percent of the votes. By 1872 their percentage was down to 54 percent, and in 1876 they lost their majority, earning only 44 percent of the popular votes.[12]

10. 353; Gordon B. McKinney, "Southern Mountain Republicanism and the Negro, 1865-1900," *Journal of Southern History* 41 (Nov. 1975), 493-95. M. LeB. to Andrew Johnson, Oct. 1, 1865, Papers of Andrew Johnson.

11. McKinney, "Southern Mountain Republicanism and the Negro," 502-503; Allen W. Trelease, "Who Were the Scalawags?" *Journal of Southern History* 29 (Nov. 1963), 445-68.

12. McKinney, "Southern Mountain Republicanism and the Negro," 497-98; McKinney, *Southern Mountain Republicans,* 32-33, 42-44, 81.

After the debacle of 1876, Republicans decided to mine the bedrock of their support, the unadulterated Unionism that the war had revealed and tempered with blood. Mountain Republicans backed away from equality measures as far as they could, while still giving lip service to pressures from the predominently black party members of the lowlands. Their new strategy was built around a military model, a "party army" to lead them to victories.

What made this model of party discipline so appealing and effective in the mountains was that it recalled the war experience — the efforts of Unionists to organize to protect themselves. It also recalled Unionist slogans, since many of their political opponents were men they had fought during the war. Leaders often declared that they were once more fighting "enemies of freedom." "Rebel" was used as synonymous with Democrat. The party-army rhetoric had a special appeal to the old Unionist soldiers who still nurtured hatred of Confederates. When Grant was running in 1868 and 1872, the link between wartime service and party loyalty was obvious and compelling. "I was a Union soldier born in N.C. and this is my home," one mountain Republican wrote. "Gen. Grant was my commander and I will do my level best for him at all hazards." The most effective election device that several mountain Republican political leaders discovered was a reunion of the veterans of the war. As one leader wrote, "There is a large amount of enthusiasm on the subject and if properly conducted will be one of the best things imaginable for our party."[13]

Thus the passions of the war and the allegiances and memories it evoked remained significant forces in shaping the politics of the mountains even after the conflict. The other major gain of the war, freedom for the blacks, remained in the mountains, not a rallying point, but a source of difficulty, a subject to be manipulated. Throughout the last part of the nineteenth century, the mountains remained dangerous places for blacks. Lynching was a frequent occurrence, and mountain Republicans could be found who justified it. And when at the instigation of some mountain Republicans, but over the objections of most, the 1890 Lodge voting bill was debated

13. McKinney, *Southern Mountain Republicans,* chaps. 4–6; James Padgett, ed., "Reconstruction Letters from North Carolina," *North Carolina Historical Review* 19 (Jan. 1942), 75–76.

in the Senate, constituents reminded the party leaders of the dangers of boldness in protecting blacks. Republicans lost five of their eight congressional seats. Although factors other than the Lodge bill were involved, Republican politicans quickly began to announce their opposition to Federal involvement in local elections. Between 1890 and 1894 new leaders took over the party in the mountain states, and they recognized the need to drop race-related issues and to focus on economic development instead.[14]

Shelton Laurel politics were untouched by the dilemmas of larger mountain Republicanism. There were no blacks in Shelton Laurel, and the people cared very little about national issues or programs. They focused on their valley and voted Republican unanimously. It became a subject of comment in 1910 when two Democratic votes were cast. The mountaineers had little reason to care for Democrats of any variety, especially since Allen and Keith had been Democrats. Their loathing of Jackson's party could only have been nourished when they attempted to gain something from the national government to compensate them for their sufferings.[15]

In 1869 eight widows from Shelton Laurel petitioned Congress for pensions. A recently enacted law allowed unmarried widows of soldiers to collect eight dollars per month and children under sixteen to receive a smaller amount. Only five of the eight petitioners had been married to victims of the massacre. The other three had apparently lost their husbands at other times.

They did not stand alone as supplicants this time. Governor W.W. Holden, several other state executive officials, and members of the North Carolina legislature added endorsements to their petition. The Senate Pension Committee was impressed, as they were intended to be, for the petition recited a lurid story of husbands fighting "for the old flag until overpowered." It described Confederate soldiers "with orders to kill old and young, especially little boys saying that 'pigs would make hogs.'" The age of the youngest victim

14. McKinney, "Southern Mountain Republicanism and the Negro," 506–508. McKinney concludes that most mountain Republicans favored the Lodge Bill but then describes the ways in which the party quickly adopted a new course after it was badly beaten on this issue.

15. Glendora Cutchell, "Shelton Laurel History" (typed family history, based on information from Bill Shelton).

was said now to be eleven, and the children were described as tied together with their fathers, "led out and brutally murdered." Worse than that, the wives and mothers were now allegedly present at the scene, begging for mercy. And there was more, for the helpless women were whipped as they watched "their husbands and children dying in their sight, and their dwellings in flames." Their only bitter consolation was hearing their loved ones exclaim, "They kill us because we are loyal; we die for our country."[16]

Time obviously had elaborated the story of what happened at Shelton Laurel in January 1863. The pitiful scene had become even more grisly and embellished with patriotic fervor. The victims had become soldiers who fought for their country, the Confederates even more savage than they had been at the time.

Yet the story did not sound unbelievable to the Senate committee. Peter Van Winkle, a senator from Appalachian West Virginia, and his associates announced that "the committee find the facts in this case sustained by abundant proof, and regarding the petition as one worthy of the favorable consideration of Congress, recommend that the prayer be granted and report a bill accordingly."[17]

The bill passed in the Senate without debate. Perhaps Van Winkle was able to persuade his colleagues that the mountain Civil War might indeed have spawned such horrors. Perhaps also the continued concern about the lives of Unionists in the South trying to prevail in Reconstruction encouraged favorable action. While Van Winkle was no radical (he had been an early opponent of Andrew Johnson's impeachment and voted against strong civil rights legislation), he clearly knew of the nature of the Civil War in the southern highlands and his colleagues in the Senate accepted his views.

But other currents than support for Reconstruction and continued willingness to pay for wartime tragedy were in the air. It was becoming clear to some that peaceful reconciliation might require forgetting, not compensating, wartime atrocity. When the Shelton Laurel petition reached the House along with several other pension bills, it was quickly tabled and sent to committee. While pensions

16. *Report of the Committee on Pensions,* 40th Cong., 3d sess., Serial Set 1362, Rept. 233.
17. Ibid.

for 1812 and Revolutionary War soldiers and descendants received assignments that promised quick action; the widows' petition went to the Committee on Invalid Pensions and did not emerge.[18]

The Shelton Laurel widows did not give up. Immediately they or their representatives began to gather more material to support their position. A neighbor who had been a major of U.S. Volunteers gave a statement certifying "that he has resided near the homes of the petitioners for many years, and knows the facts set forth to be true." Colonel David Fry was contacted, and he insisted that he had enlisted the victims in a company he organized in mid-November of 1861. The company had tried to march to Federal lines at the time but had been unable to do so because of the proximity of Confederate troops. He had therefore told the men to return to their homes and "hold themselves in readiness to start at any time that he should notify them." Fry was sure, he said, that the men were in the army at the time they were killed.[19]

With this additional evidence at hand, a senator from North Carolina reintroduced the petition for the pensions in January 1874. His name: Augustus Merrimon. If anyone could describe what had happened in Shelton Laurel, it was Merrimon, for he had first sent Vance the report of the murders. He had talked to witnesses and gathered the data for the prosecution of Keith. For four months in 1863 he had been involved in the investigation of the incident. Support by a senator who knew so much about the case suggested that this pension application would have first-hand backing from an informed and important man.[20]

The petition was sent to the Committee on Pensions and within two weeks the committee made its report, submitted by Senator Morgan C. Hamilton of Texas. As was the case five years earlier, the report described the murders, taking some of the allegations of 1869 as relevant to the petition. This recitation, however, had none of the passion of the 1869 report, and the events were presented with arid objectivity. The report cited the new evidence that had been gathered. And then Hamilton slowly withdrew the hopes built in the first part of the report. The neighbor's testimony on behalf of the

18. *Congressional Globe,* 40th Cong., 3d sess., 1252, 1326.
19. *Report of the Committee on Pensions,* 43d Cong., 1st sess., Serial Set 1586, Rept. 44.
20. *Congressional Record,* 43d Cong., 1st sess., 433.

widows was branded "hearsay." Fry's testimony was accepted but then made worthless by the assertion that "so long a period intervened between the date of enlistment and [the death of the men] as to raise the presumption that they had abandoned all intention of trying to make their way to the Federal Army." It was admitted that the earlier committee had "made a favorable report, setting out the facts very fully, which seem then to have been sustained by abundant proof." This committee was not going to be persuaded by the earlier report, however, because "the proof now before the committee is very meager. Nothing in fact is established beyond the enlistment of the men." What about the murders? According to the committee, they appeared "to have been so notorious that no one who has written or petitioned in behalf of [the] destitute widows and children seems to consider it necessary to furnish proof of the fact. No one testifies to the capture and execution of the men, not even the petitioners themselves, though witnesses present on the ground." The committee therefore, despite unctuously stating that the men were "doubtlessly loyal men and patriotic, and their melancholy fate excited the sympathies of all in behalf of those they left destitute," rejected the petition.[21]

The one thing indisputably known by the people of Shelton Laurel — reported in three major newspapers and subject to an intense investigation by two North Carolina governors, underlying thirteen indictments in the state local courts and basic to a major opinion of that state's highest court, noted with special care by the compiler of the Civil War archives and surely etched in the memory of a serving United States senator — had thus been banished into limbo by the sophistry of a Texas senator. Its existence might be summoned as the cause for condolences, but not for compensation of the victims. The massacre itself was not proven to have existed! But Hamilton was not so dedicated to proof as to require evidence for his assertion that the men had given up trying to get to the Federal army. That was based on a "presumption."

The report of the committee was not the last word. The Senate had to accept or reject the committee's recommendation, and Senator Merrimon would have the chance to respond to Hamilton's allegations. On January 22, almost the anniversary of the murders, Ham-

21. *Report of Committee on Pensions,* 43d Cong., 1st sess.

ilton made his report. Merrimon said nothing. There was no debate. The Senate agreed unanimously to postpone the petition indefinitely. There would be no payment to the Shelton Laurel widows.[22]

So far as is known, Merrimon never explained, never apologized, for his silence in the face of Hamilton's report. Apparently he was no longer very interested in the atrocity he had uncovered eleven years earlier. Perhaps he felt that introducing the petition was a sufficient act of sympathy for the people who had once touched his life. Perhaps he was trying to keep that part of his life behind him. He had in fact come some distance from the time when he was a young lawyer attending circuit court not far from Shelton Laurel.

By 1874 he was one of the most important men in North Carolina politics and was accommodating himself well to the political forces in the state. And by then those forces were strongly conservative, fighting against Reconstruction reforms, taking power away from blacks by force when necessary. Merrimon swam with those currents and had done so as early as 1867. Then he had resigned a judgeship rather than enforce the orders of Union General Daniel Sickles. He became a hero of sorts for this act, and taking hope for statewide influence, he moved away from the mountains to Raleigh and became active in the Democratic party. He had acted as a manager of the impeachment proceedings against Governor Holden and had defended accused KKK members without accepting a fee for doing so. He had been the party's nominee for governor but lost narrowly to Republican mountaineer Tod Caldwell. By 1873 he had won election to the Senate, where he would fight vigorously against the 1875 Civil Rights bill and in favor of removing Federal troops from Louisiana. The Civil Rights bill, he asserted, would "contravene the natural law of races . . . hybridize the races and produce to a material degree, degeneracy and extinction of race." He fought the Federal government's presence in the Bayou state because he believed that "every reconstruction act which was passed by Congress was absolutely null and void and in violation of the spirit and letter of the Constitution."[23]

22. *Congressional Record*, 43d Cong., 1st sess., 843.
23. *Dictionary of American Biography*, vols. 11–12; *National Cyclopedia of Biography*, vol. 9, 270–71; Hamilton, *Reconstruction in North Carolina*, 543–49, 585–87, 594–95; *North Carolina Supreme Court Reports*, vol. 111, 568; vol. 114, 690.

At such a time in his life, memories of atrocities against mountain Unionists must have been clouded indeed. To fight for compensation for them would only revive hatreds and retard the restoration of control of southern affairs to conservative hands. He had a career to protect, ambitions to nourish. He may have projected something like what the future in fact held for him. Although defeated for reelection to the State in 1879 (his old friend Vance won), he was compensated with appointment to the state supreme court and by 1889 he was chief justice of the North Carolina supreme court. When he died in 1892, eulogists spoke of the nobility of his character and the high offices he had held.

Two of the speakers at his memorial service would look back to the days of the mountain Civil War. The world they recreated in their eulogies recalled Merrimon's courage and devotion to duty. The mountain war they evoked was one in which bands of outlaws from both Union and Confederate armies pillaged and killed, and "lawlessness and bloodshed" were rampant as these outlaws tried to "demoralize and destroy the community." Through it all Merrimon, "with full knowledge that [his life was] in danger," "with great courage and firmness, as well as prudence and ability," sought to bring justice to "the mountain fastnesses." These were appropriate memories. In that time Merrimon had acted admirably, uncovering an atrocity he might have ignored or avoided. Time had eroded the specifics of his role in the Shelton Laurel tragedy, however, and no one recalled exactly what he had done beyond being courageous and prudent.

They knew that he had gone on to great service to the state and the nation and had been to them "one of the best and truest and noblest men . . . at all times . . . possessed of the courage of his convictions . . . essentially a man of the people." He had also been, they said, a judge known for his "courtesy, promptness, impartiality and fairness"; a United States senator who "so bore himself that none could doubt that he had no other end in view than to serve the best interests of his state and country," and through it all "an anxious and earnest seeker after eternal truth."

Merrimon's eulogists were especially impressed with how far he had come from humble origins as the son of a poor mountain minister, farmer, and merchant. He was too poor to attend school as a child, but his ambition and his thirst for knowledge drove him for-

ward to the position of lawyer, then senator and judge. Marked with
energy and vigor, he had forged himself into a man who was "punc-
tual, punctilious in following rules . . . thoroughly acquainted with
the rules of evidence," with a mind that was "honestly logical." The
eulogists might also have noted how passionately opposed to drinking he had become, as they did note his commitment to the public
schools of the state as avenues for advancement.[24]

Merrimon had indeed come far. Born and raised in a place known
for its wildness, its excesses, he had escaped them in himself. He had
renounced the "drunkenness, the ignorance, superstition and the
most brutal debauchery" that he had observed as a young mountain
lawyer. He had defied the brutal lawlessness of the Civil War mountains by insisting that the courts and legal process mete out punishment for the murders in Shelton Laurel. The pension petition must
have seemed a minor matter in a career that included grand accomplishments. Even in this matter he may have felt satisfied, for in at
least offering the petition, he had given the mountaineers due process. Let them seek justice someplace else. There were so many
more important things to deal with. Why regress to such a place—
such a dangerous place—such a small place? Merrimon looked
away and went on to grander things.

In Shelton Laurel, meanwhile, life went on. The failure of their
pension claims meant that the only immediate reminders of the war
were the graves on the hillside and the changes that came in the way
people lived and who they lived with. Surviving casualties of war
were taken in by kin who cared for them. Mary Shelton, who had
been whipped and hanged for a time by Keith's men, lived with John
and Matilda Shelton, who were pretty well off by Shelton standards
and could give her special care. She needed it, for sometime between
1860 and 1870 she had gone insane. Martha White, who had married a Shelton, was now back living with her parents. In January
1863 she had been beaten and tied by the neck to a tree. James Shelton's family, who had lost their father and two of his sons, was now
headed by Patsy Shelton, who kept up the place with the help of two
older girls and their younger brothers, John and Calvin, who had
been too young to fight. The family stayed together, sustained by

24. *North Carolina Supreme Court Reports,* vol. 111, 568–73; vol. 114, 690–92.

kin and love of the place. James Shelton's grandson "Bud" is still there.

Some of the general patterns of life were shaken a bit. By 1870 women headed seven Shelton households. There had been only one in 1860. There were about ten more kin living in households they had not been born in than had been the case in 1860. Perhaps these were signs that the war had disturbed the pattern of life, but the change was small. Folks in Shelton Laurel generally remained poor. They raised large families. Girls and boys who were probably kin married each other and had children. People farmed and hunted and cared for the house and stayed on their land. History had wounded them, but they endured. And now history had moved on, and they were left with their lives.[25]

25. Manuscript Census, 1860, 1870, Madison County, N.C.

APPENDIX DATING THE MASSACRE

The record provides two conflicting dates for the massacre. The Shelton Laurel widows in their petition to Congress give the date as January 18, 1863. Lawrence Allen gave his friend A.P. Gaston a description of the events surrounding the murders that would make the date sometime between January 25 and February 1. I have accepted the earlier date for the following reasons.

First, the weakness of the Allen testimony. Allen helped Gaston write his recollections in 1892. At the time Allen was trying to reclaim land from people who were using the story of the murders to discredit him. He thus could have been remembering poorly after the passage of almost thirty years. He also would have had reason to want to misdate his recollections to demonstrate that he could not have been responsible for the killings. This possibility is weakened a bit by the fact that at no point did Allen ever directly deny his part in the murders and, in fact, his recollections describe the joint expedition he and Keith participated in that almost certainly led to the murders. Still, he may have known that he could not deny his part in the atrocity and so sought to cloud the record by introducing another chronology.

Allen was not above this sort of obfuscation. During the war he tried to cover up his recruiting racket by writing to a fellow officer that some men in the unit might claim to be "unlawfully detained" and that the governor might take action to have them released. He was painting the picture of trying to help Vance with the investigation into charges that Allen himself was the cause of "unlawfully detaining" these men. Furthermore, Allen was familiar with the game of misdating letters. He got a letter from Keith that the latter had misdated by over a month in order to cover his tracks on the recruiting enterprise.[1]

Second, Allen's 1892 recollection is faulty. He claims that in early January 1863, Kirby Smith in Knoxville sent him orders to punish the Unionists who had raided Marshall. At that time the commanding officer for East Tennessee, with headquarters in Knoxville, was not Smith. It was Henry Heth.

Third, the Shelton Laurel widows had nothing to gain by lying about the date of January 18, and they surely would have remembered such a day.

Fourth, the January 18 date would fit with supply requisitions signed by Allen and Keith and a subordinate in Knoxville on January 12, 13, and 14, 1863. These supplies could have been the ones drawn for the punitive expedition against Shelton Laurel. Of course, the same supplies could have been drawn at this time for a late January expedition, but it would have been unusual to draw supplies so early for an expedition that would take the Sixty-fourth on only a two to three days' ride from Knoxville.[2]

Fifth, correspondence between Governor Vance, General Heth, and General W.G.M. Davis discussing this expedition to punish the Marshall raiders begins describing the expedition on January 20, 1863. Intriguingly, in a letter of January 20 to General Heth, Davis seems to be responding to some special concern about Allen's unit. Davis volunteers the information that "Col. Allen's Sixty fourth North Carolina Regiment and the men of his command are said to have been hostile to the Laurel men and they to the former for a long time—a kind of feud existing between them."[3]

1. See Allen to Garrett, June 4, 1863, A.J. Morey to Garrett, mid-June 1863, Governors Papers, Zeb Vance, Box 166, State Archives, Raleigh, N.C.
2. Military Records of Allen and Keith, National Archives.
3. *OR,* ser. 1, vol. 18, 810–11, 853–54, 867.

Sixth, since Allen recalled being with Keith on the fatal expedition and the other records prove that Keith was present at the killings on January 18 and also note Allen's presence, it is highly likely that the proper date is January 18, 1863. The records supporting this picture date from 1863, although the first ones to mention January 18 itself are the pension petitions of 1867. Still, a document written within four years of the event seems preferable to one written twenty-nine years after it.

It is possible that the later date is the correct one. The first direct reference to the massacre is in a letter by Merrimon to Vance dated January 31. Vance acknowledged receiving this information in a letter of February 2. There was a telegraph line between Greeneville, Tennessee, and Raleigh and someone could have gotten the story out of Shelton Laurel and gone to Greeneville with it for passage to Vance on the last day of January.[4]

For this to be the case, it would have to be true that Keith and Allen came into the valley after the expedition itself had left and committed the murders more or less on their own. Neither one of them was above this sort of freelancing. For the reasons given above, however, the earlier date seems more plausible.

The establishment of the January 18 date does present another difficulty, however. The evidence for the deaths of Allen's children comes from the 1892 source. The sequence of events arising from that source is the following: January 26, Allen and Keith ride into the valley. January 27, Allen hears of his children's plight and rides to Marshall. January 28, Allen in Marshall buries the children and returns to the unit. Sometime after that the murders occur. I believe that the murders followed the children's deaths because the evidence is strong that Allen was with Keith at the time of the murders—a fact never denied even by Allen himself. If he entered the valley on one day and rushed to Marshall the next, there would not have been time to capture the prisoners, hold them for a day or two, and then kill them. The most plausible resolution of the conflicting evidence about the date is thus the one presented here. We can accept Allen's sequence of events, but should follow the chronology of the other sources.

4. Merrimon to Vance, Jan. 31, 1863, Governors Papers; Vance to Davis, Feb. 2, 1863, *OR,* ser. 1, vol. 18, 881.

INDEX